UNLEASHING YOUR
INNOVATIVE GENIUS

UNLEASHING YOUR INNOVATIVE GENIUS

HIGH SCHOOL REDESIGNED

DEBORAH OLATUNJI

NEW DEGREE PRESS

COPYRIGHT © 2020 DEBORAH OLATUNJI

UNLEASHING YOUR INNOVATIVE GENIUS

High School Redesigned

ISBN   978-1-64137-375-3 *Paperback*
        978-1-64137-289-3 *Kindle Ebook*
        978-1-64137-291-6 *Digital Ebook*

For my little sister, Testimony, who showed me why education must change; and my future children for whom I pray the system will be different.

TABLE OF CONTENTS

———

INTRODUCTION 9

HOW TO UNLEASH THIS BOOK 19

PART 1. HOW TO CONQUER THE CLASSROOM 23

CHAPTER 1. WHY SHOULD YOU REWORK IT? 25

CHAPTER 2. BREAKING THE "AVERAGE JOE" MENTALITY 33

CHAPTER 3. THE PROGRESSIVE POWER OF I 45

CHAPTER 4. THE UNCONVENTIONAL TRUTH ABOUT PASSION 55

CHAPTER 5. WHY YOU SHOULD CREATE YOUR OWN ACCESS 73

CHAPTER 6. FAILING TO SUCCEED: HOW TO FIX YOUR GRADES 83

CHAPTER 7. HACK HOMEWORK: CREATING INDEPENDENT STUDIES 95

PART 2. HOW TO RETRAIN YOUR MIND 109

CHAPTER 8. PUBLIC (SCHOOL) ENEMY NUMBER ONE...TEACHERS? 111

CHAPTER 9. CURRICULUM WARS: WHO IS RESPONSIBLE FOR THE DAMAGE? 123

CHAPTER 10. SERIOUS INQUIRIES ONLY: THE DEBATE ON CAREER READINESS AND REPRESENTATION 135

CHAPTER 11. "LATE" IS BETTER THAN NEVER 151

CHAPTER 12. CHARACTER-BUILDING: THE POWER OF
GRIT   161
CHAPTER 13. THE CONSEQUENCES OF "WE":
INTEGRATION THAT EXCITES   173
CHAPTER 14. HACK COLLEGE ADMISSIONS: ENOUGH
SAID.   185

PART 3.   HOW TO UTILIZE THE OUTSIDE WORLD   199
CHAPTER 15. FINDING THE CHAMPION WITHIN   201
CHAPTER 16. WHY YOU SHOULD INCLUDE YOUR
PARENTS   217
CHAPTER 17. VITAL TOOLS YOU WON'T LEARN IN
SCHOOL   231
CHAPTER 18. WHY YOU NEED A MENTOR AND WHERE
TO FIND ONE   251

CONCLUSION HACK LIFE! UNLEASHING GENIUS   267
FEATURED POEMS   271
ACKNOWLEDGEMENTS   283
APPENDIX   291

INTRODUCTION

———

Spark ideas.

Embers within us that lead to further discovery and inquiry of self. The brush of light when a lost thought turns into a life-changing movement.

These are powerful visuals and something each of us hopes will happen in our own lives or our children's lives.

Spark is that moment of light and energy; it's the mere beginning of things. Ideas are the currency of innovation and ambition, the incentive that drives us to want more.

More innovation.

More collaboration.

More conversation.

More inclusion.

Is this what we're doing in today's school environment?

**

The time to find this spark in yourself usually happens sometime during the long, grueling years that are the K-12 education system.

Think about it: from as far back as elementary and as recent as your current school experience, what were the most captivating parts of your education?

Like second grade cooties, I must wonder, has learning ever been contagious to you? Did that spark spread?

At the conclusion of sophomore year, I faced some tough realizations:

School is not a place where I feel my ideas are heard.

High school is the last time I have to figure out what the heck I want to do with my life.

College must be better than this, but how will I survive for the next two years?!

One day, in the tenth grade, I went to my younger sister's elementary school and saw an image placed by the entrance. The sign read, *WELCOME, CLASS OF 2030!* I was shocked—I would be twenty-eight years old when this class graduates!

I was shocked for two other reasons beyond my obvious age increase; one, I graduate high school in the year 2020, so these kindergartners will be graduating high school a full ten years after that; two, I thought to myself, *how crazy will the education system be then, a decade after I've graduated?*

Now, 2030 is just around the corner. We are at the cusp of a new decade...I'm not getting any younger.

And neither are you.

With this daunting revelation, I started to deconstruct how school impacts me and who I am beyond academics.

What does school mean? How have I developed a purpose through it? How best do I learn to recognize and achieve self-discovery from true learning?

Adults tell us that everything we learn is for our own good, even though we haven't really explored what we want our own good to *look like.*

But what if you were able to explore that idea?

What if you were given the opportunity to take control over a certain number of hours during your academic year? If you had thirty minutes each school day to do whatever you wanted:

- How would you use that time?
- How would you measure the success of your project?

Don't worry if you don't have all of the answers right now. When I considered those questions myself, I realized that I didn't even know what I'd do with all that time.

**

Given my passion for education reform, I set out to talk to some people in the field: Angela Duckworth, Ellen Stofan, Sir Kenneth Robinson, Tasha Taylor, Garry Johnson III, and Senator Elizabeth Lockman, among others. I also wanted to hear from fellow students: Morgan Rollins, Miracle Olatunji, Jerome Foster II, Bryce Fender, and Andrew Yu. These students have been hacking their own education—redesigning their experience—to see what they would do if they had this little bit of control.

But why me?

Why am I writing this book?

I have seen the state of education through different lenses: in terms of access, opportunity, and connection.

Without interacting with my own education in an unconventional way, I don't think I ever would have been able to call myself a dynamic public speaker, award-winning poet, youth innovation board member, bold activist, and Black female founder. Nor would I have been named one of the 100 High Schoolers America Needs To Know About in 2019.[1]

---

1   Workforce Career Readiness. "100 High Schoolers America Needs To Know About Class of 2019."

For me, the intersection between learning and community has grown a network of twelve freshman year high school friends to over 800 professional connections across the United States and internationally (specifically Jordan, Portugal, India, Mexico, Colombia, the U.K., Kazakhstan, the Philippines, Nigeria, Ghana, Peru, Liberia, Canada, and more).

I feel the United States' education system is currently under a state of delayed progress. We as students often find ourselves bored in our classrooms; information bounces off us as if we are walls. My philosophy for redesigning education is inspired by that and my role in the decision-making process for a youth-led organization called GripTape. My fellow board members and adults in the room have given me a seat at the table, along with a platform to share my ideas and perspective as a high school student.

There is certainly something empowering about working with an organization that positively impacts students just like you, a person filled with creativity and boldness.

I have seen firsthand how, when young people have control of their learning environment, it can catalyze their view of education and themselves.

I've started to see new elements of myself. With this kind of exposure I have become a leader and learner.

From ages three to nine, private school education was the only world I knew. With that basis of close, learner-centered education, my first year of public school was a culture shock. I didn't realize how different those two environments were in cultivating the student experience, which I will bring with me to college in the fall.

What I do know now is while my own personal education outlook has been through the lens of private, public, and public charter schools, my interaction with the legislative side of education policy enabled me to want this change. Yes, change. By identifying various problems with all three schools, I thought about the students who never had school choice or whose choice ultimately altered their access to education.

**

Think about it this way: if you were given thirty minutes of every school day from kindergarten to senior year to solve a problem you are interested in, you would have had 57,600 minutes, 960 hours, 40 days—almost six full weeks of time.

How would you spend this time?

Does the thought of having autonomy, or self-determination, over that much of your school life **terrify** or *excite* you?

No matter which, know these feelings are shared among the 56.6 million students currently in the elementary, middle, and high school systems.[2]

Learning is an integral part of who we are.

---

2   National Center for Education Statistics. "Fast Facts: Back To School Statistics (372)."

It never ends, but that is not what school teaches you. Right now, there is a start and an end to the process: kindergarten through senior year.

Unfortunately, this way of thinking can kill our innovation cycle. If you knew at the beginning that an idea wasn't going to turn out as you had originally planned, would you have pursued it in the first place?

Your answer is probably, *"No, are you kidding me?"*

Learning is just like that. It's running with an idea and seeing what it teaches you. It's trying to solve a problem and being led to new ones. This is not how education currently is. Instead, it often discourages students to take risks and penalizes making mistakes.

We don't know exactly where the effort of problem solving is going to take us, but the journey and people we meet along the way make it worthwhile. That's how I've been able to connect with and learn from so many diverse minds from around the globe. The value of learning lies in never stopping the innovation cycle; it is the continuous questioning of the world you know and ones you have yet to explore.

**

I want to transform the education system for my generation and my future children.

Education is not something that can be shoved into a standardized curriculum over eighteen years. Education happens over the course of a lifetime, through supported learning and putting ideas into action.

What does that look like in this book? Here's a quick preview:

- Founder of 360VR Technology and University of Delaware student, James Massaquoi's idea of setting your floor before raising your ceiling. "You must design the floor plan of your end goal before working your way up the elevator to the fourth floor." **What is the best strategy for sky-high goals (like starting a radio show or writing a book) and where does the courage come from to take either the elevator or the stairs?**

- Sir Kenneth Robinson's philosophy of passionate connections to information learned rather than mindless memorization.[3] *Even if I can memorize twenty words in fifteen minutes, what does that say about my ability to effectively communicate my ideas to a group?* **How can you spin the practice of rote memorization to help you in the long run?**

- Wisconsin high school student Morgan Klug's interaction with "shock value" and how her experience in an apprenticeship has helped her completely rule out a certain career path now, rather than figuring later out it wasn't for her. "[Apprenticeship] is a really interesting way to give students an upper hand. If they're interested in something, then give them an opportunity to

---

3   Robinson, Ken. "Do Schools Kill Creativity?" TED video, 19:22. Posted February 2006.

partner with a corporation, a company, or even a small business, to work on something they are potentially interested in going into in the future." **When should you tap into the experience economy or the abundance of experiential resources, and how do these learning experiences contribute to your traditional learning journey?**

In this book, I offer a road map for hacking personalization in your education experience. You will discover what to do with your newfound flexibility and ultimately how to transform your learning journey wherever it may take place.

YOU DON'T HAVE TO BE A STUDENT TO TAKE ACTION WITH THIS BOOK.

I intend for the ideas here to resonate with teachers, parents, policymakers, educators, guidance counselors, and others who care about enhancing the future of our education system. Read How To Unleash This Book for direct chapter references and more.

By the time you finish reading, you will be ready to...

DO AWAY WITH busy work — how do you replace worksheets and boredom with action and fervor? By taking on personalized learning practices, you will find what it means to be an active and independent student.

DISCOVER what individuality is — how to define your brand and find value in individualized learning. By examining other students' paths into their passions, you will be empowered to branch out of tradition and into innovation for your own path.

DIVE INTO the power of student agency and creation of hands-on approaches to your learning — how to utilize outside resources to upgrade your high school experience. By practicing the tips in this book on the three core parts to unleashing genius, you will no longer see your passions as difficult endeavors to save for when you "grow up."

Now, let's unleash genius!

HOW TO UNLEASH
THIS BOOK

———

Treat this book like a menu. Here are some suggestions to help you get the most out of the experience:

HIGHLIGHT WHAT YOU INTEND TO GET OUT OF THIS BOOK

Understanding what you want to learn is a fundamental hack. This book is about how you can create your own high school experience and ultimately tap into your unused potential. Let's kick it off with this tip: **Write down the questions you want this book to answer for you.** Then go find those answers.

Look at each chapter as a standalone, insightful hack.

Don't let the length of the parts determine whether you will start or finish this book. Read the chapters that grab your attention, push you to ask more questions, indulge you in finding those answers, and motivate you to act. No one chapter will transform you into an innovative genius, but each chapter can impact your journey to taking charge of your education.

USE THE STRUCTURE AS A GUIDE

The format of this book is composed of three parts: how to conquer the classroom, how to retrain your mind, and how to utilize the outside world. Many chapters are connected in some way, but don't let the structure hold you back.

POINTS OF INTEREST

For the most part, this book is written as if the reader were a high school student. The objective of this kind of diction is to showcase a rarely acknowledged group that now has their moment to shine. Most works on education have youth in the backseat instead of the driver's seat of the process... not here. The specific audience is high school students, but everyone is welcome to join and contribute to the conversation. These groups include:

Teachers/Educators: Chapters 1, 6-10, 17-18

Parents: Chapters 1, 8, 13-16, 18

College Students: Chapters 1, 3, 10, 12, 14-18

Politicians: Chapters 1, 3, 14, 17

Even if you don't fall into any of these categories, my hope is this message of innovation and action will spur you to disrupt the current face of your field whether it's engineering, medicine, real estate, technology, computer science, what have you. After all, we are all students of life; the students who read this book and use this early opportunity to discover experiential learning rather than digest information are the ones who will end up as the leaders of their fields.

ACT ON WHAT YOU READ

There is a huge difference between knowing information and putting knowledge into action. You will only become more innovative by taking steps to change up your current routine. Be sure to go through the takeaways and lessons at the end of each chapter and respond to the call to action. The only way we can discuss education reform is by first knowing what the conversation is about and how to address the problems discussed. It is, in my opinion, better to act on the Call To Action portion of a chapter than to skim an entire part.

PART 1:

HOW TO CONQUER
THE CLASSROOM

CHAPTER 1

WHY SHOULD YOU REWORK IT?

———

"Without ambition one starts nothing. Without work one finishes nothing. The prize will not be sent to you. You have to win it."

— RALPH WALDO EMERSON

Let me begin by saying this: we are all consumers of education.

Yes, you read that right.

We are all consumers of education.

Whether you are at the beginning of your freshman year of high school or in the last month of your senior year or even well beyond high school, you have experienced, used, and perhaps even *enjoyed* school at some point in your life.

Often when we think about consuming something, it's either food and drink or media like television or movies.

However, as consumers of education, you probably haven't had the same kind of choice you enjoy with other things you consume. That's where this book comes in. You may not have the ability to seize full control of your education due to traditional standards, but now you can understand how to reshape your education. I am here to show you how!

**

At the start of the tenth grade, I absolutely hated history. I struggled with civics as a freshman and didn't see the value in learning about a bunch of dead men who wouldn't have cared about my existence. As a Nigerian-American teenager, I quickly realized that people of importance only looked a certain way. Our study objective was to acknowledge the contributions of one group that significantly disenfranchised the rest. It felt isolating; these characters were presented to me as "ground-breaking visionaries," but they were all in the same condition as my three-hundred-page textbook: pale, stale, and outdated.

This bothered me. It didn't seem like this course cared about race and inclusion.

World history appealed to me because I thought the material would focus on pioneers of different skin tones and from different cultures. However, I caught on that, like many classes in high school, the course content didn't match my expectations or resemble real life. World history was supposed to mean including everyone, but we never studied Africa beyond slavery.

Instead, the course focused mainly on Europe's unquenchable thirst for conquering unsuspecting nations. Christopher Columbus sailed the ocean blue *on that fateful day in 1492.*

The rest is history.

On my first test that semester, I received an outstanding fifty-nine on a test. My first high school F and a perfect representation of my distaste for the subject. F for the fact I still vehemently hated history and F for feeling failure, despite knowing that one test could not shape the entire marking period or the year.

Plus, my teacher loved giving group projects and making sure we interacted with different classmates at every possible opportunity, which often resulted in collective groans and unhappy sighs.

But why is any of this important?

Who cares if I got a failing grade and had to deal with the hassle of frequent group work?

To my surprise, World History ended up becoming my favorite class my sophomore year…and I never wanted to miss a single second of it.

How did that happen?

After receiving that first low grade, and without much of an idea for an action plan, I embarked on a personal journey to hack this subject and make improvements. I had to find out why the material mattered and connect it back to my world.

The alternative was allowing that single grade to define me and shape the course of my year.

First, I examined my situation: I knew in order to take United States History at a higher level the next year, I needed to pass the class with a ninety-five average. This was an ambitious goal, especially coming off a fifty-nine, but I set the goal and nullified any self-doubt and worry I had. If it wasn't helpful, it didn't get to stay in my mind.

Then, I asked myself what I *wanted* to get from the class: if reading about colonizers didn't spark my interest—which they didn't—I would play a game with myself to motivate and excite my mind about the unavoidable study process. I over-emphasized the name pronunciations, gave the "characters" nicknames, and treated them as interviewees as I studied. As it turns out, pretending to be an investigative journalist is much more interesting than sleepily reading a textbook! Who would have thought?

Vasco da Gama became a person of interest in his successful quest for India.

Marie Antoinette, headlined with her famed supposed phrase "Let them eat cake," paid no attention to the tough situations of the poor, which mirrored the realities of the modern world. By drawing contemporary parallels to the apathy in France then, I examined the effect of the elite becoming more elite.

Maximilien Robespierre, a lawyer who rose to power during the Reign of Terror[4], showed me the extremes of what can happen when only one opinion is considered valid. I learned that while speaking with others makes developing stories stronger, unconventional methods were often met with fear due to ignorance. Breaking through one's bias toward progress required reaching out a hand, not a place in line to the guillotine. Capital punishment aside, this history class transformed when I established connections to the real world.

Finally, I actively sought out help from my access network. My peers also took this course, whether they adored or despised it, and I figured since we were all it in together we should act like it. I diligently completed homework assignments and asked for clarifications to test questions I hadn't gotten right the first time. I used to rely solely on teacher reviews from previous students, but then I started to connect with my teacher as a real, empathetic person.

Building that relationship was key to turning my hatred of the class into something I loved.

You may have experienced something like this; how did you handle it?

---

4   Andrews, Evan. "Reign Of Terror | History, Significance, & Facts." Encyclopædia Britannica.

There are ways of using your peers in the wrong way to just get by in the class. You could choose to buy into the false belief that because the first test was not a victory, then the rest of the school year will be the same way. Neither one of those options is helpful or positive—not if you want to successfully rework your education.

You can instead alter your situation and achieve a personal goal that might seem impossible.

You can take even the most traditional curriculum and mold it (and your response to it!) to fit your interests.

You can rework the system, by using your network and connecting with others to achieve a common goal.

But why should YOU rework it?

You should rework it because four years is a long time to be miserable, bored, and disengaged in your own education. These last four years of secondary school create the foundation for what the next four years of your life will look like, and the years after that, and the years after that. And ultimately, the life you create for yourself!

You should rework it because school can be much more enriching than it may feel like right now. Even within the restrictions of our education system, there are a few distinct ways you can add some much-needed flavor to even the blandest of classes.

**

Imagine waking up to the same meal every day, with no variety, freshness, or special of the week.

What does this symbolize?

This analogy might closely resemble your current classroom. An outdated menu may be your textbook or the course material, the meal is the school year, the chefs are your teachers, and the kitchen is your classroom. While you may not be able to change the menu, the meal, the chefs, or the kitchen, you do have the power to impact how you comprehend the contents, how you respond to material, how you engage with your teachers, and ultimately how your classroom experience engages you.

Education and learning are two distinct aspects of this metaphorical buffet to which you have been invited. The education aspect shows you just the options without considering personal taste or allowing for customer suggestions.

The learning part of your meal, however, leaves room for changing the way certain meals are prepared. There's some flexibility for the consumer. It is up to you to create the meal you desire most and work with the chefs, food, and kitchen at your disposal.

This book will show you the recipes for self-invention and increased agency in yourself.

TAKEAWAYS & LESSONS:
- Seek knowledge to connect with the course material and beyond it.
- The difference between education and learning is flexibility. Learning can mean one thing to a friend and something entirely different to you. You're both looking to get an education, but the methods you use will vary.

CALL TO ACTION

I challenge you to turn a boring and seemingly pointless subject into a series of interviews or opinion pieces to help you connect with the material. These may not be the best methods for you, which is why I encourage you to try them out and see what works!

CHAPTER 2

BREAKING THE "AVERAGE JOE" MENTALITY

———

"The current world doesn't need creative people; it needs people for the workplace who show up to work on time."

— TASHA TAYLOR

Are you doing everything you can to ensure you are an Above Average Jolene?

Ever since I was a kid, I had to choose for myself whether I would be status–quo or status-*yo*. (That's Spanish for "I").

With a battle between comprehension skills to memorizing colors like *azul, rojo, y naraja* and greeting phrases, like *me llamo*, in the first grade, I always had a competitor. From the moment my brown eyes felt the harshness of light in that NYC maternity wing, my identical twin sister represented a constant reminder that a world of difference floated away from my tiny hands' reach.

Growing up with someone who looks exactly like you can create a kind of conflict within yourself, which you cannot seem to shake. I know firsthand from daily comparisons that feeling like the copy of someone else doesn't do miracles for your self-esteem.

The idea of being average has occupied my mind longer than I can remember. When you're little, you're just trying to figure out how to tell time and when you'll eat next. Or tell a story from recess in Spanish.

The high school experience can change a person's point of view, identity, and outlook on the world.

Oftentimes, I have found myself on a purpose quest, searching for what it means to have an impact and bring my own goals to fruition. I've felt average in my activities before, from the dulling homogeneity of high school, the never-ending cycle of rise, school, sleep, repeat, to college preparation.

It's easy to feel as if nothing particularly makes you unique. You may begin to question why you need to stand out in the first place. By slipping into this hole of thought, I became aware of my weaknesses, what I considered to be strengths, and my weak attempts at goals. Most high school students go through this mental game on an hourly or daily basis, trying to determine their self-worth through mundane activities that make them feel *like everybody else*.

I am here to tell you that you must break through this slimy "Average Joe" mentality in order to become an Above Average Jolene.

There is a significant difference between utilizing your imagination and exercising your creativity. Creativity plays a large role in what it means to be an "Above Average Jolene."

The innovation consultancy company Creativity at Work defines creativity as "the act of turning new and imaginative ideas into reality. It is characterized by the ability to perceive the world in new ways, to find hidden patterns, to make connections between seemingly unrelated phenomena, and to generate solutions."[5]

We need creativity to learn how to make ourselves above average.

This definition should, in my opinion, align with classroom curriculum objectives to show students the value of nonconformity and innovation. Additionally, creative thought in critical situations can help you to see a solution from a place of personal design and open a pathway for even more creativity in the new structure.

You can use your imagination in the process of getting this done, however the folks at Creativity at Work note that if you have ideas but don't act on them, you are imaginative but not

---

5   Naiman, Linda. "What Is Creativity? (And Why Is It A Crucial Factor For Business Success?)" Creativity At Work.

creative.[6] You must *actualize* the ideas you generate in order to experience an impact.

For example, I had the idea of writing a book, which made me imagine the process, the cost, and the efficiency. However, the phrases, "I am thinking about writing a book" and "I am writing a book and it is about _____" are very different stages of making the goal happen.

I am imaginative for my ability to think of communicating my ideas through a physical project, but my creativity to *pursue* the project is what distinguishes me from an "Average Joe" to an "Above Average Jolene."

I also want to point out that the progression from average to above average currently lies in the metrics of the traditional school system. Calling students these words helps educators to filter through the system, tagging and bagging students by performance. Or, by giving letter grades as restrictive labels to how a student performs.

For example, an A for "You're excellent, above average, a star;" as opposed to a D, "You're lost, unteachable, and failing." However, these two statements can be spun to mean something of personal value and aid elevation through our individual traits and ideas.

**

---

6   Ibid.

In my first quest for outlets of creativity, I joined a motivational program for students of color to amplify their portfolios with intriguing college courses.

Through the TeenSHARP program, an organization focused on supporting Successful, High-Achieving, and Reaching Potential (SHARP) students, I was able to take college classes on topics that piqued my interest.

I also was taught by my first Black instructor, Garry Johnson III, through his entrepreneurship course, ENTR156: From Ideas to Action. He stressed the importance of this concept, so my peers and I understood the breadth of opportunity for Black, Asian, and Hispanic students—to see that nothing could limit our potential, regardless of the color of our skin, to see that we weren't just average.

He also shared with me an important lesson from a notable interaction with one of his teachers. During the first week of school, his biology teacher gave him a homework assignment to bring in a hat of any kind.

He immediately thought, "I know! I'll bring my SpongeBob hat. The one with the eyes on it!"

Like many high school students, Garry woke up late that morning and rushed to school without realizing he had left his hat behind.

Walking into class, he looked around at the rich variety of hats his classmates adorned on their heads. Panic seeped into his mind. "I forgot my hat!" Rushing over to his friends, he asked if anyone brought an extra hat with them.

"Sorry, no."

"No, Garry! I only brought my own."

With a brief look of dismay, Garry realized there was only one thing he could do. Running back home wasn't an option.

He created one out of origami instead.

Creative right? Innovative even.

The moment came when his teacher waltzed around the classroom, clipboard in hand, checking to see if his students had completed the first assignment.

When he finally got to where Garry sat, his teacher looked at him in disbelief. "Where's your hat?"

The paper origami work of genius stared back at the teacher, in shock of the mockery to deny its identity as sensible hat-wear.

Garry points to his quick solution on his head. "It's right there."

The teacher replied with a stern "No. Where's your hat?"

Garry continued to insist the origami masterpiece was his hat. His teacher frowned at him and said, "That doesn't count." He proceeded to mark Garry's grade slot with an X, a zero of out five completion points.

My thought after hearing this emotionally scarring story might resemble the one you're thinking of now. *But Garry did complete it; he just did it in an unconventional way!*

This experience made him not want to fold paper ever again; as a freshman, this was his first grade and he was now "failing" biology after the first week of school!

He had to explain to his parents how, when he used his creativity to solve a problem, someone hindered him and said no.

After reflecting, he looked back and learned you must persevere in order to be successful. He also realized being different and thinking outside-of-the-box was something above average even though he received a below average score.

The experience emphasized to Garry the indispensable value of diversity, in the way everyone brought in a different kind of hat. What they brought represented a piece of them, something which should be celebrated. He had the most unique product and it still failed him.

Sometimes in life, your creativity will not be given a platform to thrive. Sometimes if you are different, you will be shunned and treated differently. It certainly is not a cure-all solution to the question of how to be successful.

This is a reality for many students, especially those of color. Garry didn't feel like he had to be like everyone else; his biology teacher represented a group with a numerous population. Most of us know them as haters. But much more specifically, we will call them the **squelchers of creativity.**

These are people who insist on preserving a dull sameness in us. We all have them in our lives, but it's ultimately up to us to break from the mold and design the masterpieces of which we are truly proud; to boldly embrace the various aspects that make us who we are and who we strive to represent.

In fact, you should—like Garry—use your creativity to solve problems! You stand to gain more from your ability to tackle situations from unique angles as opposed to following the same path paved by others.

**

It is also important to have multi-dimensional traits through choice and courage.

Tasha Taylor, graduate of Delaware State University, spoke with me about how scheduling works at schools. As a recent generation of required classes one through five and then having the "freedom" to choose the sixth one, it will take time to deviate from a one-size-fits-all framework and allow students to create effectual content of their own.

As Lily Dalile, former contributing writer at the *HuffPost*, put it at age fourteen, "I understand that memorizing is the fastest way to get good grades, get into a good college, and get a job (which we equate with a good life). But we are being educated for the promise of money."[7] Learning should be driven through specific interests, not solely on requirements.

You can become above average by adding to your educational experience in a unique way. As a co-founder of a non-profit that runs on student agency, Tasha's perspective on desperately needed change compelled me to write a specific story on the idea of a free curriculum—one not as restrictive as it is right now. Imagine a world where you could take an experimental math class or combine biology with theater.

Think about how empowering it would be to yell, "I am the powerhouse of the cell!" in a slow, loud, and dramatic voice to an audience.

Educational drama supports learning about a combination of both the course objectives and personal goals. While acting out the cell cycle and key components of the biology curriculum would increase student interest, it would also help students in understanding cell biology.

In an interactive math class, I could explore the complexities of Algebra 2 and Pre-Calculus and turn them into project-based assignments. Instead of finding the mean or standard of deviation for the number of students who passed or failed a quiz or test, you can use the experimental nature of math to compare world markets and explore the intricacies of geometry in architecture.

---

7   Dalile, Lily. 2012. "How Schools Are Killing Creativity". Huffpost.com.

No matter the direction you decide to take your ideas in education, it's important that you come to terms with them and do not hold back in expression. Even if they seem to be "average," developing innovative alternatives to common approaches comes from your personal touch!

The only moment you become a "Joe" is when you ignore the artistic voice inside of you.

You are not an Average Joe because of the creative potential you already have and can grow; however, you must ensure you are taking steps daily toward becoming the Above Average Jolene that you are destined to share with the world.

TAKEAWAYS & LESSONS:
- The grade on an assignment or test does not equate to how skilled you are, or who you can become.
- Expressing your knowledge and understanding for a subject or topic takes many different shapes, forms, and hats.
- You don't have to follow the status-quo to achieve your personal goals. You do have to redesign or rethink your approach to a situation though if it does not fit how you best perceive the world.
- Find different ways to enhance your individuality because when you are comfortable with yourself and your process and want to grow, you will be unapologetic about your passions.

CALL TO ACTION
I challenge you to create an educational drama. Here's one way how:

1. Take a topic from a subject you love or struggle with.
2. Choose the characters. Create a script to share the story of how the process works.
3. Act it out!

Example: Cellular Respiration from Advanced Placement Biology[8]

Characters: The Cytoplasm, The Pyruvate, Pyruvic Acid, Glucose, The Mitochondrion, The CO_2, The ATP Synthase, The Citric Acid Cycle, 38 ATPs, NADH, FADH

Act It Out:

Scene 1: Glycolysis.

Scene 2: Citric Acid Cycle.

Scene 3: Electron Transport System.

Show your teacher what you come up with! You can also create a mini comic book instead of a live action theater presentation.

---

8   Rein, Abi. "Cellular Respiration - Lessons." Tes Teach With Blendspace.

CHAPTER 3

THE PROGRESSIVE POWER OF I

"The most common way people give up their power is by thinking they don't have any."

— ALICE WALKER

The empowerment that comes from achieving a project by your own merit is second to none. With the obstacles and challenges that come along, by the end of your journey you would have put every ounce of passion into the goal. Empowerment begins with the I Factor, recognizing that while a goal may seem tough, your determination and focus will help make it happen. "I factor" simply refers to your streams of confidence and what propels you to map out your vision of success.

You will experience these moments of setting goals and achieving them throughout your time in high school and beyond.

In fact, the process of unleashing genius starts with having confidence in Player Number One—you.

∗∗

By seeing how others activate this power, you can learn how to discover your own.

Melinda Kassandra Lopez, a native of Sleep Eye, Minnesota, completed both her high school curriculum and an associate degree in nursing simultaneously. By her calculations, she will obtain a bachelor's degree at nineteen and be a licensed medical doctor by twenty-four or twenty-five—three years earlier than her prospective peers.

"I really love what I do. I have a passion to live my life in service to others, to advocate and be a leader for others through health care. I have my next ten years planned out," she says.[9]

An avid reader and dedicated softball player, Melinda notes her goals: (1) to empower women and (2) help people in any way she can.

From her experience, there are a few lessons you can take away, even if dual enrollment seems out of reach:

1. Find a goal that aligns with your values and who you are.

---

9   Smith, Alex. "Minnesota Student Will Graduate With High School Diploma — And Nursing Degree." Star Tribune.

2. Know you are not just a student. You are more than a student and your desire to solve a problem in various areas in your life will show that.

3. Utilize your network! With big goals comes great responsibility. While Melinda's story seems impossible, she points out that she would not have kept up with her goal without active communication with her network.[10]

Your network is a supportive and motivating group of people who propel you to think beyond yourself and your goals to find your true values.

You can find your network in other diligent students, your teachers, or outside mentors. However, the drive must be ignited within **you** for any of this to happen.

**

You can also activate the progressive power of I from looking at the practice of homeschooling.

Homeschoolers usually get a bad rep when it comes to their balance of social interaction and academics, but if you think about their education style, they have a pretty sweet deal. In 2016, the National Home Education Research Institute reported that 3.3% of American students have the home-school experience.[11]

---

10 Ibid.
11 Ray, Dr. Brian D. "Number Of Homeschoolers In U.S. 2017-2018 Home School Growing." National Home Education Research Institute.

But what does it really mean to have school in the comfort of your home?

Homeschooling is a progressive movement around the country and the world, in which parents choose to educate their children at home instead of sending them to a traditional public or private school.[12]

The idea that students should have a personalized approach to learning and understanding key concepts is the message *all* schools should promote. Research shows students have fewer issues with mental health and peer pressure when they activate the "I Factor."[13]

The learning design firm, Getting Smart, believes there are many benefits to personalized learning—especially through promoting student voice and choice, a flexible learning pace, and the ability to learn anytime, from anywhere.[14]

This is not to say you should withdraw from your public or private school and switch to hitting the books at home. I share these studies because they encouraged me to have a more active instead of passive role in the choices surrounding my education.

⁕⁕

12   Martin, Jamie. "Homeschooling 101: What Is Homeschooling?" Parents, 2012.

13   Horowitz, Juliana Menasce and Nikki Graf. "Most U.S. Teens See Anxiety, Depression As Major Problems." Pew Research Center's Social & Demographic Trends Project.

14   Poth, Rachelle D. "Personalized Learning Experiences: Why? And How?" Getting Smart.

In the seventh grade my older sister, Miracle Olatunji, went through the process of being homeschooled. My three other siblings and I went to public schools.

There are a lot of misconceptions around the home-school experience, so I want to debunk them and make some clarifications. Now I know that Miracle is not the only person who has experienced the home-school model, but many home school students can relate to some areas of her experience.

Miracle went to a school where she would only attend classes on Mondays, then receive homework and assignments to be completed by the following Monday. Not only did she have to build up incredible self-discipline by completing a week's worth of homework on time all year, she also had to learn how to engage herself with her peers and ignite interests outside of school for the remaining six days of the week.

Now, years after having the experience, Miracle has grown into a dynamic person. Her potential came to life when she had time to reflect on what she was learning, connect with others on a deeper level, and build self-awareness and time management skills. This past year, she published her first book, *Purpose: How To Live And Lead With Impact,* and was mentioned in *Forbes* as a high school senior for founding OpportuniMe, an application that democratizes student opportunity. She has also become a worldwide public speaker. This, my friends, is the power of God and the "I factor" in a very real way.

Who would have thought a shy, "reserved" kid would go on to find her purpose and create ways for others to find their own as well?

From studying the model of home-school education, I realized I can utilize their techniques in my public charter school education. Here are some effective skills you can use to approach school like a homeschooler.

- Faith
- Follow-through
- Forgiveness

Students who have these three skills usually tend to have a solid grasp of their learning, their network, and the "I factor."

1. The *faith* — believe in yourself and your ability to achieve prominent tasks that are paramount to your success. This sets the trajectory of your goal, by choosing the problem you want to solve and planning out the steps to find the answer or more questions. You need to believe the result of your confidence doesn't end in a letter grade, academic percentage, or calculated grade point average. A better result comes from the expansion of your network, acquisition of new skills, or new interest in topics that align with your passion.

Sometimes progress is better measured through guidelines you create for yourself. For Melinda, she mapped out a few years. In order to actualize her goals, she had faith in her connections to help her have the confidence in herself to get the job done. If you can't believe in yourself, search for communal faith.

2. The **follow-through** — a dedication to accomplishing tasks is crucial for the faith that will push you to complete your main goal. You must find what is best for you in terms of *work ethic, communication, and time management.* Without some sort of grasp of these three key skills, it'll be tough to find fulfillment in pursuing a passion that is outside of the constrains of "normal" extra-curricular activities.

You may enjoy chunk-work, block-work, or scatter-work. Discover what works for you.

> *Chunk work is doing your assignments in massive quantities. For example, in terms of schoolwork, if you have eight classes and homework in every class with only eight hours to accomplish the work, you can do three tasks in three hours. Then, another three in the same amount of time and the last two in final two hours. Blockwork is the complete opposite. With blocks, strategy is better than speed. You can block off time in two-hour pieces, digging deep into separate pieces of two subjects at a time. Scatter-work is block-work but scheduled throughout the week rather than in one day. I use the blockwork method to get started and transition into scatter-work as the week moves along! If none of these methods fit, design your own!*

3. The **forgiveness** — be kind to yourself. This will enable you to have comfort in self-created breaks, or "me time,"

and moments when you need to take a few steps back to understand what you need to accomplish and *why*.

Whenever I feel discouraged about not reaching a set goal, I think of soccer legend Mia Hamm's words: "Failure happens all the time. It happens every day in practice. What makes you better is how you react to it."

Even the most successful people in the world—athletes, musicians, and business owners—emphasize the importance of being able to acknowledge flaws in their routines without punishing themselves for it. The next time you attempt your goal, you will know how to refine it to propel yourself closer to that championship, elite concert, or final closing deal.

For you this means reworking your learning experience. By channeling the purposeful confidence in your goals, desires, and plans, you can become an ***unstoppable genius***.

TAKEAWAYS & LESSONS:
- Even though it is much easier to conform to a set of rules, you can chart your path.
- Focus on playing to your interests, instead of allowing an expected plan of study to shape your learning.
- Utilize faith in your ability to fully actualize your ideas. Design a follow-through to make those ideas reality. The three keys are work ethic, communication, and time management.
- You can have confidence and the willpower to achieve, but make sure you forgive yourself when the original plan

changes. In those times, reflect on your concerns and worries to help define the next steps you need to take for progress.

CALL TO ACTION

I challenge you to make a three-year plan. In this plan, write down a couple of goals by year (Year 1, Year 2, and Year 3) you want to make happen. Be sure to add which kind of workflow you will use to accomplish them and who will be keeping you accountable. Then, check your plan after a month and edit it as your interests and priorities evolve. You can do these eleven times a year and start outlining with my chart below!

💡YEAR ONE	💡YEAR TWO	💡YEAR THREE

CHAPTER 4

THE UNCONVENTIONAL TRUTH ABOUT PASSION

———

As I look into the depths of my mirror
I stand there in all my black girl magic and beauty
And I wonder
Who am I?

I. AM. 1968.
I am arguably the most world-changing year history has
  ever had to sit through
Flying to
New lands and new territories
Bloody wars against Vietnam and lost pieces of glory
From anti-violence to sports discrimination
Just five years before, Martin Luther King had a dream
When in 1963
He proved that words can move a generation
Now, stay with me,
1968 was a year of waiting
Waiting for change

Waiting for violence
Waiting to bring black voices to silence
April 1968
Dr. King was shot in the right jaw
A couple seconds later our hero did fall
But his legacy was only just beginning
The white oppressors thought they were winning
But little did they know
That we would no longer keep sitting...

**

In today's growing world, many more students have the opportunity to go to school and feel empowered by an education experience. The possibilities of "firsts" and "lasts" help create a timeline for how this journey will play out. From your very first steps to the final walk across the stage at high school graduation, we all unknowingly digest copious knowledge.

So, where does this information go? What is the purpose of it and how can understanding its function help us follow our passions?

I asked myself this question at age seven, even though I did not have the full answer.

To me, passion meant loving something so much you turned it into a career. But even at that young age, I knew there were certain passions that wouldn't lead to a prosperous lifestyle or have a "get-rich-quick" technique handy.

So, what is the objective of knowing your passion for a subject anyway?

One method is using the knowledge you learn to spark an interest in other areas of your community. I found genuine interest in both learning history and making history after hacking my World History class. It mattered to me because for the first time, the people of prominence weren't just one color. Their mission toward equality made me realize how uninformed I was about my own history.

**

...Uprising
Martin Luther King, Jr. was not the only man that died that
    day
The rage that shook the country
On the news of Martin's death
Caused the anti-violence movement to halt itself
and fall out of breath
Lootings, arson, violence, and death
How can we move past this
How can we recommence
April 4, 2018
Marked fifty years plus, of us
Still living in fear
Fifty years of us trying to move past this feeling of hatred
Of each other, of each color
Being filled with envy and pride
Just like the bullet
That killed King that night

Our progress is not preset, and people can't process that
prospect
If we want change, it has to happen today
Rewind to 2 months before the assassin was assessing his
asset
A march through Memphis was felt and met
Civil rights activists marched tall and with their heads to
the sky
Looked death in the face and said, "Oh hi,"
With sandwich boards proclaiming the freedom they sought
Their workplaces were unjust
And it was time that they stood up and fought
Calling black men boys
And treating white men with poise
$2.35
White men get higher pay
$1.70 for the black men
Hey, that's twenty cents more than a movie ticket back in
those days
"I AM A MAN"
And I demand more for what I labor
1,300 black sanitation men marched to bring justice in their
favor
Tired of the maggots and rain
Their hardship
Was strengthened with their stand
Leading to two black men being crushed to death in the
pouring rain
Sixty others were injured
And a sixteen-year-old Larry Payne was shot in disdain
The last speech Dr. King ever gave was the very day before
his own death

On the march in the city of Memphis
Get this
The police brought tear gas and beat people out of their
senses
Census
So many people died that year
It was a wild roller coaster
That took people up, down, and around with fear
RFK took a bullet
By a man who was mentally ill
Coulda, shoulda, woulda been avoided
Sit him down and give him a pill
MLK, JFK, and RFK all
Died young because of men who were slaves to violence…

**

From my new-found appreciation for the past, I sought to perform this knowledge with my community.

In December of 2017, my twin sister Dorcas found the final registration deadline for a speech contest. The topic was Dr. Martin Luther King, Jr.

We were supposed to write a speech, poem, or rap which captured our personal reflection of the effect of Dr. King's legacy on our lives. I had less than a month to create a piece!

Now in class, the only time I ever heard about King, other than the question of why we didn't have school on a "random" Monday in January, was that disruptive day of assassination—April 4, 1968. Other than those two occasions,

Black History did not have a prominent role in my learning curriculum.

I loved writing poems and history was starting to intrigue me, so I chose to tackle this project with every ounce of creative passion I had to offer. The experience taught me that even the most important details that make me who I am won't always be part of a curriculum objective.

So there I sat in my basement for hours, combing through history in my Google tabs like Ritz crackers in a ten-roll, family-sized box. No matter how salty, I had to devour them to feel content and aware.

I learned about events from the '60s to the present. I felt ripples of shock from what I found.

Large pockets of sadness were kept tucked away by government and far from intervention's reach for a long time. For example, the controversies of the Vietnam War with our troops, civil liberty issues of ethnic minority groups, and the reign of racially insensitive groups like the Ku Klux Klan who sought to terrorize and kill black people. All events that rarely came up in class discussions.

I uncovered history about how 1,300 black sanitation workers marched through Memphis in a strike, holding signs that read "I AM A MAN" after two other black men were crushed to death by a garbage truck in search of shelter from the rain.[15]

---

15 Estes, Steve. "'I am a Man!': Race, Masculinity, and the 1968 Memphis Sanitation Strike." *Labor History* 41, no. 2 (2000): 153-170.

I was shocked to read these men were only earning an average of $1.70 per hour but sometimes as low as $0.65 cents, for their labor as opposed to white counterparts making $2.35 per hour. [16] The black men also worked long hours with no overtime pay and no paid sick leave. [17] They demanded recognition of their dignity and humanity. This was a time where token integration quietly replaced public segregation in Memphis. [18]

After three hours of digging through all I'd encountered in a power sweep of the last sixty years and reflecting on barrels of injustice, I started trying out creative phrases, writing words that made some coherent sense. The poem "I AM" was born.

Research empowered me; I truly enjoyed rewriting and reciting my creation to myself and to my family and friends. I practiced over ten times before the semifinal and finalists' round.

That night, as I stood in all black on the stage, I thought about what the process had meant to me. There were no grades, no tests, and no affirmation of my success other than what the judges chose that night.

No do-overs, no retakes, and no corrections. Despite all this, I learned so much more about black history than I ever

---

16   Broderick, James A. and Jill A. Broderick. "February 12, 1968: Black Sanitation Workers Strike In Memphis." Rhapsody In Books Weblog.

17   Brown, DeNeen. "'I Am a Man': The ugly Memphis sanitation workers' strike that led to MLK's assassination." Washington Post.

18   Morland, Kenneth J. "Token Desegregation and Beyond."

would in the twenty-eight days that scratch the surface of our impact. The proof is online.[19]

After that night, I continued to share this poem with my community. It made me uncomfortable at first. However, when I saw the tears of the much older audience who had been taken back to that time in their lives and embraced the disheartened individuals who came up afterwards, I realized how important this message was.

I finished third in the competition in January 2018. My love of this experience led me to pursue more avenues for poetry and speech. The following year, I created a second piece called "Color-Blind" and won first place.

Like a domino effect, I developed a passion for learning and creating history as well as writing and researching. These became effective tools for public speaking and award-winning poetry pathways. As a bonus, I ended up winning $2,250 across both years.

With this experience, I was able to talk to fellow community members about the New Jim Crow[20] and understand the effect of having race-based conversations rather than passively digesting information and nodding my head at the history being discussed.

The term Jim Crow refers to "a series of laws in United States history that enforced racial segregation in the

---

19   VisualImagesMedia. "I AM | Deborah Olatunji." YouTube, July 2, 2018.
20   Teaching Tolerance. "Introducing 'The New Jim Crow.'"

South. The laws existed from the time the Civil War
(1861–65) ended to the Civil Rights movement nearly
100 years later. In The New Jim Crow, author Michelle
Alexander explores complex questions about the crim-
inal justice system and the history of race and racial
justice in the United States."[21]

I ended up public speaking multiple times. My favorite
speeches were with a college theater performance group
called the Women of Consequence at the University of Delaware and the Power and Change Conference at an all-boys
Catholic school. I also started interacting with an action-ori-
ented community advocacy group, Coalition to Dismantle
the New Jim Crow. By going outside traditional topics learned
in class and diving deeper into a past I wanted to know more
about, I became an avid consumer of knowledge—without
being force fed irrelevant content to which I could not relate
or derive insights. **Then, I went on to produce knowledge
of my own.**

**

...Now there were great people who positively shook the
    country
Like Honest Abe over 100 years before
Men and women who grabbed injustice by the reins
Trying to bring it down to the floor
The Arlington National Cemetery
Holds so many bodies filled with promise
That in seconds their change

---

21   Alexander, Michelle. "The New Jim Crow Context." Course Hero.

Was buried in a casket
Instead of assassins, let's raise children who will be asked
the right questions
No Child Left Behind in poverty or on the list of
dishonorable mentions
Instead of firing bullets, let's raise builders who will help
bring up our country
Instead of hate, we'll put up our hands

In the 1968 Summer Olympic Games in Mexico City
Johnny Carlos and Tommie Smith took a black panther
salute
During the national anthem
We all bleed the same dark red
But they beat us vile blue
The only color that shines is the white
We wonder what. can. we. do.
I AM THE YEAR 2000, *where Peter Norman of the same*
Olympic Games was denied his right
To march with the alumni Australian team
Saying he didn't deserve it
After supporting John and Tommie decades before
His name went unnoticed, turned against
And despite qualifying 18 times they never gave him their
token
What good is it
If we cannot compete and say our minds
Peter died in 2006 and six years later they
finally apologized…

**

Even if writing or history aren't for you, there are other subjects with compelling alternatives to discover and implement into your own routine.

Zach Jones, the creator of Dual School, a youth empowerment program that gives students three hours during the school week to create projects of their own, spoke to me about the power of student-focused learning.

He said, "We forget how cool learning really is."

We really do and it's a shame. Learning can either be an unapologetic embrace of empowerment, or an obstacle between empowerment.

After spending four years studying at Stanford, Zach concluded, "If you have no desire to learn after age eighteen, you will not want to learn!"

Immediately upon hearing the word "learning," I have a slight inner cringe. My brain has been wired to associate learning with a rigid concrete building, as opposed to a center where creative thought can thrive. That's why taking "early action" in high school about coming to terms with your access is so important!

If you are a math lover, or even if you hate it or don't mind it, Zach has a question for you.

"Would you rather take a test on geometry or build a chair for someone in need for a final grade?"

Most people might respond to this question with an unfazed acceptance of option one, instead of trying out the possibilities to see if building a chair can work to help a person in need. This is a direct scenario of how to use mathematical methods to construct a real product which people can either enjoy or loathe.

Many students will see this question and think, "I simply don't have time to build a chair" or "Where can option two go on my resume?"

I know because these thoughts used to be my own. However, this idea reinforces the concept of solely **doing** for a destination, rather than for an impact.

But even if you choose geometry because that is what you genuinely are curious about, what's stopping us from applying geometric principles to the innovative nature of architecture and learning why essential projects must take certain paths for success?

Personally, I would build the chair. I've always been curious about wood and nails, I guess.

The unconventional nature of turning learning to action is what will propel you to personalize what you intellectually consume.

**

...I AM 2002
Still in recovery from the 9/11 attacks
On August 14, 2002
The changemaker standing right in front of you
Was born
And welcomed into a new world
That needed love, justice, and racial reform
I AM 2017
And this year was not the finest
From D.C. to the very lack of kindness
Repeat
We were repeating history
With black athletes taking a knee
Right before the glory
But now,
Now we're undeserving
Apparently, we should be grateful
GRATEFUL FOR WHAT?
For the many years that America kept snoring
Saying civil rights and matters of inequality were too boring
To fix
For that, they have no decision
But against their gun laws they make no hesitation, take no
*   fall*
After all, it's what they want to use
To kill us all
Maya Angelou wisely proclaimed:
You may shoot me with your words
You may cut me with your eyes
You may kill me with your hatefulness
BUT STILL, STILL. I. RISE!
We won't keep quiet because

I AM 2018
A year of change
And like Fannie Lou Hamer said
I'm sick. and tired. of being. sick. and tired.

This country needs to open its eyes
And stop all these gunshots from being fired.

**

For my art-inspired friends, this second scenario deals with graphic design. Zach gave his students two different options: creating a movie poster or designing and screen-printing T-shirts. This last option would give students complete authority in the design process and the capability to start their own company selling T-shirts. Which one would you choose?

A pair of his students, who were hesitant or shied away from this model of learning, did not "pass" their first checkpoint in their idea path. Not many people showed up to the presentation for their project of interest. This could have made them give up or change their project idea.

However, instead of seeing the situation as what could have been a C on a grading scale, their Dual School team encouraged them to reflect on what went wrong, so they could try again. And try again. And try again until it changed their trajectory of what it meant to "pass." When they connected with what they wanted to convey, the number of times they "failed" turned into lessons rather than let-downs.

Zach encouraged them to look at the business portion of learning on how to create your own clothes, whether they sell or not. Either way, you would be seeing how to manage a business, assist customers, design something worth paying for, and generate revenue.

In the words of queen Oprah Winfrey, "Forget about the fast lane. If you really want to fly, harness your power to your passion." The best way to take flight is by learning *why* something you do is important. The "why" is so much more important than the "where" when it comes to discovery.

- Why did they march?
- Why does that screw fit here and not there?
- Why do I mix certain dyes to make the colors and layout for the clever design?

Finding your passion is not an easy task and they tend to evolve as you experience more life. However, if you can connect the link between the activities and subjects you do and why, you will recognize a desire to know more about how to learn more beyond surface level.

TAKEAWAYS & LESSONS:
- Choose to discover why you have an interest in a topic, rather than where it will get you. The passion behind your interests will help you become more open to stretching your mind and learning new ideas.
- Engage in unconventional ways of understanding a concept. You don't have to use a textbook to learn. The more experiential, the better!

- List three topics you have never explored but want to make the time to dig into:
  - 1.
  - 2.
  - 3.

After you have chosen three, create an action plan for how you will learn more about each topic. You can do so by listening to podcasts, watching documentaries, reading unassigned books, and discussing these things with your friends and family. Include when you intend to learn each one and for how long. You don't have to pursue all three simultaneously and can spend as much time as you desire before investing in another topic.

Your Action Plan:

- Then, understand that being a "nerd" is never a bad thing—an investment in your passions and ideas will help you in creating your own access on your path.

CALL TO ACTION

I challenge you to become a life-long learner. Find a problem you want to solve or an issue you haven't had the chance to explore in-depth. As Zach Jones said, "Don't wait for someone who may not be there to give you direction." Create new knowledge from your experiences.

CHAPTER 5

WHY YOU SHOULD CREATE YOUR OWN ACCESS

———

"Our deepest fear is not that we are inadequate. Our deepest fear is that we are powerful beyond measure. It is our light, not our darkness that most frightens us. We ask ourselves, 'Who am I to be brilliant, gorgeous, talented, fabulous?'"

— MARIANNE WILLIAMSON

Access means acknowledging barriers and creating the solutions to run through them. In terms of removing obstacles, access deals with your approach and strategy for victory. Victory can be achieved through many different avenues with access. Networking and perspective are some of the keys to creating your own path.

Your access is how you choose to look beyond your plights as a student and work past them to generate success, whether that is an academic problem like grades or a social issue like a wardrobe.

You need to know why self-initiated access has so much power and how to channel it into your passions and ideas.

**

My learning journey has been unique for a few different reasons.

I grew up attending private school and never knowing anything outside of my 250-person school from grades K-4. I knew about the world and trends, but I did not experience interacting with people of different beliefs, cultures, and ideas until I started attending public school. I thought my little Bible buddies and siblings were all the people I would need to make a tangible difference.

To say the least, my line of thinking was limited. I didn't fully understand public education at first or why anyone would *not* want to wear uniform to school.

I got my only taste of "wardrobe freedom" during the fifth grade, my first year at a public school. There were six different fifth grade classes and 913 little people running around in the building throughout the school day. I can proudly say to this day I survived, but it came at a perilous cost— my sense of style and fashion taste proving themselves nonexistent.

My past wardrobe mistakes are just one example, however, of how I identified a newly existing problem and sought to find the solutions.

On a more serious note, the decisions made in elementary and middle school seem to have a momentary effect on your past self. Sometimes, it can appear difficult to create your own access if you didn't have or understand it in the past.

Increased access can even feel overwhelming or undesirable at a point. My stress striving to be a pioneer in my interests resulted in hours of reversed productivity and self-doubt. I had to overcome.

Either way, you have probably recognized at some point you desired control.

Attaining this access requires an identification of the drive that will help you brainstorm how to transform your own pathway.

**

I could say that the process is as simple as one word: networking.

> **Networking** is the practice of interacting with profes-
> sionals in an organized space. Think about it like a
> party for your ideas—a place you can talk about them
> and find people who will want to celebrate it along with
> their own. Unlike the ending of a regular party, where
> you and friends head home after tons of dancing, a

networking event is a launchpad for where the connec-
tion begins. After meeting these people, you can com-
municate virtually by reaching out to them on LinkedIn,
by email, or a phone call. LinkedIn is to Instagram for
business as networking is to partying with intention.

Earlier in March, I decided to meet up with a friend to discuss this idea of becoming a trailblazer with the help of a community. He was also an assistant instructor and completing his third year of college for the course ENTR156: From Ideas to Action, an introductory class on innovation, creation, and entrepreneurship with Garry Johnson III.

James Massaquoi, now a fourth-year student at the University of Delaware studying Business Management, has interacted with his education through humor and curiosity. As the classic class clown making jokes as early as elementary school, he quickly became close to his fourth grade teacher.

She pushed him to do more like running for class president, performing in a play, and pursing ideas that would give him more confidence. She started off as just a teacher, but then her role in his life catapulted into a mentor. This was only the beginning of James' network and his understanding of how to reach what he wanted (and didn't know he wanted) in life.

He also had his fair share of teachers who didn't believe in him. His high school microeconomics teacher told him he couldn't major in Economics and wouldn't do well in that field; now he will be graduating in May 2020 with two degrees in Economics and English, extensive experience in human relations, and as a co-founder of 360VR Technology, an emerging company that uses smart technology to protect lives.

James had to navigate between the two worlds—external support from others and the lack of it. He took on his desire for access in the topics he had interests in.

When we spoke on the phone, he painted an interesting analogy about ceilings, walls, and floors (and I can promise you you'll hear about more location analogies and metaphors throughout the book.)

Often as students, there is an increasing pressure to have staple traits of perfection and excellence. The practice of checking boxes, filling in blanks, and bubbling in correct responses appears to be a surefire way to attain "perfection." This mechanical outlook, however, affects the self-made and society-influenced qualifications generated to portray success.

James says you should worry not about "raising your ceiling, [because] it's about setting your floor."

The glass ceiling metaphor is what Investopedia calls "an artificial barrier that prevents women and minorities from being promoted to executive-level positions within an organization. The phrase glass ceiling is used to describe the difficulties faced by women when trying to move to higher roles in a male-dominated hierarchy. The barriers are most often unwritten, meaning that women are more likely to be restricted from advancing through accepted norms and implicit biases, rather than defined corporate policies."[22]

This ceiling relates to difficulties that seem too challenging to break. The big goals. The sky-high thoughts. The dreams that result in large and often time-consuming investments.

However, in the rapid pursuit for gold and glory, if there's no foundation set on what you eventually want to accomplish, everything will likely fall through like quicksand. You must design the floor plan of your end goal before working up the elevator to the fourth floor. The floor plan represents your access with support; the raised ceiling is just the goal.

In this metaphor, there is tangible action the floor setters conquer but ceiling raisers miss.

First, you must know or have a general idea of what kind of building to construct. In terms of school, find a problem in your routine and work the framework for a new solution. Those solutions may be to add more people to your blueprint or remove some extra hands, take down roadblocks by directly speaking to others about what parts you need or advice to start the job, or redirect the original idea with bigger or smaller investments in order to secure the foundation.

These tried and true approaches can be applied to almost any area of your school life. For example, taking on a group community project to advocate for a cause you are particularly

---

22   Kagan, Julia. "Glass Ceiling." Investopedia.

passionate about can turn out as intended or with unexpected surprises.

Then, it could be the case the you are missing materials needed to execute your plan. If you can get other students involved, it helps! If you need more buds, reach out! That means growing and using your network.

Finally, in the event the first floor plan cannot fulfill the intentions of your design, rework it. For instance, if your plan is to initiate 300 youth volunteers in your area, but you only get 150—half of what you expected—see how you can channel that assistance in a more productive direction.

The point of aiming high is to encourage yourself to see the endless possibilities that lie ahead—the view beyond the ceiling.

However, reaching for something does not equate to completing the task at hand. If you have no metaphorical ceiling or floor to access the end goal, you must find a way to create a backdoor. This is yet another way to create your own access.

Let's say you are trying to get an A, but your test taking results never reflect what you desire, no matter what you do. In school terms, back doors can consist of:

- Requesting a test or testing method like a video or poster presentation that fits your learning style, but also achieves the intended level of difficulty.
- Cultivating a method where you can troubleshoot the situation through a personalized testing plan.

- Hashing out the three main pathways mentioned before...
  - *Create or find a problem in your routine and work up the framework for a new solution.*
  - *Supplement for the missing materials by asking for help.*
  - *Rework your methods if the first or second or third or fourth or tenth attempts aren't working.*
  ...in order to create a method that has the same existing requirements as the ones you've learned to master (whether that's requesting collaborative assessments, different strategy lesson plans, or projects that communicate the same objective).
- USE YOUR CLASSMATES! Ask your peers for help! This applies to almost all school-related downfalls. The likelihood that another student felt the same way you do about a particular subject or topic is very high. I can give you advice based on my Delaware education, but at the end of the day there is nothing quite like advice from your hometown gals and guys.

**

Another important thing to define is what creating access really means, especially when it feels like your ceiling is caving in and the floor is nonexistent.

When I was first trying out the plan to draft a book, it was during the ease of my sophomore year's end. I saw the process as inviting and even though I'd never done it before, I knew I would utilize certain aspects of those three core ideas to build my design. The blueprint ended up pushing into my junior year, when the PSAT was the only thing standing between homecoming and the craved end of the first marking period.

However, the initial process didn't start until after midterms the following year. Before the process kicked off, I began by asking myself what I wanted to know about the topic, how I wanted to answer the questions I had, and whom to ask for their valued opinion.

Now, I'm a senior juggling this book, college admissions, and a rigorous schedule of six full class blocks. The main point is a goal may appear to have many levels of difficulty of which you don't think you are capable; however, you must create your own method for tackling it, so it can be accomplished. Even if it means spending more time than you originally planned.

I have also learned you should never measure your success by using someone else's ruler. Your floor plan will look different from your friends' and your family's and that's okay.

After all, paving the way to your own access will help you to direct others as they chart their own. You have the tools needed to victoriously achieve your goals and can do even more with a strong network. Trust me!

TAKEAWAYS & LESSONS:
- NETWORK, NETWORK, NETWORK! I cannot stress this enough. Access cannot be achieved without establishing your support community through networking.
- Breaking a glass ceiling involves setting your floor first.
- Never focus on what others think of you. In creating your own access, you must believe you are fully capable or will become fully capable. Then you will turn your dreams into ongoing actions.

- Make a timeline for yourself but don't be afraid to change the process as it realigns to your plan. Sometimes the outcome you expected is entirely different than what actually happens. Find comfort in the fact that your passions can change, just like your path to turning them into reality.

CALL TO ACTION
I challenge you to reach out to five influential people (from your place of worship, school board, news station, administration, gym club, advocacy group, poetry organization) on Instagram, Twitter, LinkedIn, or Facebook who align with the problem you want to solve.

CHAPTER 6

FAILING TO SUCCEED: HOW TO FIX YOUR GRADES

———

"If you want success, figure out the price, then pay it. It sounds trivial and obvious, but if you unpack the idea it has extraordinary power."

— SCOTT ADAM

High school can have its ups and downs. For the most part, it can feel like an overplayed drama with no end.

Even when you are reaching for the stars, reaching the ceiling can feel like the hard part. Failure is an inevitable part of aiming for success.

The dictionary definition of failure is "the omission of expected or required action." I see it as the jarring situation that occurs when you get an 89.4444 and not an 89.5 (or pretty much an 89. anything) on the 100-point scale where a 90 is an A *and* it's the end of the school year. Those are truly rough moments where you feel, "If I had only done w, x, and y, I would have been able to achieve z."

Adults talk about failure as a defining portion of a career and as a past tense event that does not occur on a monthly or even daily basis.

But what does failure mean as a teenager? How is it measured?

It's missing the mark by a seemingly small margin. It's the bad aftertaste that comes along with something less than what you expect from yourself or what is expected from you. Your academic value—commonly measured through a grade or number—is supposed to reflect the entirety of your intellectual capabilities.

Failing hard equates to a C or below to most and letting yourself down when it comes to a "big-deal" kind of outcome like your mid-year progress report or final transcript.

I want to show you that failure and success have similar meanings and takeaways. When you fail, you start the next day with the capacity to fail again or succeed. When you succeed, you start the next day with the ability to succeed again or fail. Success and failure both have temporary effects on the course of your week, month, year, and life. The reaction you provide to each of them ultimately steers you in the direction of growth as a person, student, and accomplished human being.

⁎⁎

Whenever you unexpectedly experience something humiliating, it may feel like you are trapped in a figurative box. Have you ever thought to yourself, "Can I just disappear? Can I just crawl into an underground hole where no one will see me in this moment of immense humiliation?"

This "hide-in-a-hole" syndrome can rise after a low score on an AP test, marking period average, or standardized exam. At first glance, this sensation isolates you from accepting your faults; however, it also positions you to regain lost hope and temporary happiness. By acknowledging that the bad score will not go away by getting frustrated with it, turning the anger into determination can go a long way toward a better academic result.

I say "better academic result" in this way because I believe grades are not the sole indicator of success in the real world (if at all), but unfortunately are in high school.

I have faced numerous setbacks and push-forwards during my time in high school. When I was a freshman, I remember thinking, *"When will I get to the subjects that will actually matter to me? How will I find my purpose in a sea of over-achievers who desperately want a golden A on everything they come across, myself included?"*

As a sophomore, I learned how to fail. And I learned how to fail fast.

FAST as in Frequent Acceptance of Seen Talent. What the heck does that mean?

Forbes contributor Dan Pontefract is the CEO of the Ponte-fract Group and leadership strategist who breaks down this fail–fast concept. Originating from "Silicon Valley and its ocean of startups, the real aim of 'fail fast, fail often,' is not to fail, but to be iterative. To succeed, we must be open to failure—sure—but the intention is to ensure we are learning from our mistakes as we tweak, reset, and then redo if necessary."[23]

In order to reach success, you must become comfortable with something going wrong. Instead of panicking or becoming frustrated, work through problems and learn from them. You don't allow the situation to control you because you can control your response to it.

**

In my heavy-hearted pursuit to obtain a perfect report card, I realized I'd lost my love and appreciation for learning.

So, I embarked on a path to forget grades and remember the joy I felt when a concept made real sense to me. I stopped striving for numbers and started aiming for knowledge. I constantly wanted to accept that I had the capacity to do more, learn more, and give more. It was hard to make myself believe this because for years I had been told my grades were

---

23 Pontefract, Dan. "The Foolishness Of Fail Fast, Fail Often." *Forbes*, September 15, 2018.

a clear representation of what I knew. As my AP Biology teacher always said, "Failure doesn't mean you don't know what you're doing. Not getting that grade means the method you are using to achieve needs a bit of tweaking."

There, my friends, is where the real sense of failure took off. As it turns out, failing is actually a great way to discover a passion.

"We all know how it feels to be misunderstood and criticized. To be kept in our place because we see things differently, feel things differently, and want to do things differently. But what if within the very weaknesses we're criticized for, were seeds for our greatest strengths?"[24]

—*JON MERTZ, AUTHOR OF ACTIVATE LEADERSHIP:*
ASPEN TRUTHS TO INSPIRE MILLENNIAL LEADERS

No one will ever tell you that they enjoy failing, but from the depths of a tough experience innovation and drive can be cultivated.

Gabrielle Thomas—founder of the Youth Advocacy Council in Delaware, Fellow for 50CAN, and master's Education Policy student at the University of Pennsylvania—works with students to help exercise their voices toward issues about which they care. She knows students must be at the forefront of the decision-making process, otherwise they'll inevitably lose interest in helping.

---

24 Mertz, Jon. "Activate Leadership – A Calling." Bing video, 02:22. Posted January 2015.

To answer the question of how we can help students discover their passions, Thomas says, "You have them try to answer big questions like 'What new approaches in teaching would you like to try/see?' or 'What is the purpose of school?' Problem solving is a key approach to getting students to think creatively. It's paramount to have students question their realities and be encouraged to solve problems, fail, iterate, etc. Exposure is also key!"

There is a noted difference between failing and learning from it and failing and sprinting in fear from the results.

For example, if public speaking is something you have little exposure to, the first time you engage in it the nerve-wracking thought that your words are gibberish will either suffocate your ability to try again or mobilize your recognition of a second chance. When I first started pitching my ideas at entrepreneurship contests, I was frightened at the idea of speaking on-the-fly and completely improvising my message. However, I learned how to use problem-solving to smooth the experience. Pitch after pitch, I was able to hone my improvisation skills.

Feeling afraid can feel like failure. But instead of being paralyzed I turned to problem-solving, which then led me to realize I have a passion there after all. Now public speaking is something I could see myself doing for the rest of my life.

You need to see the problem in the way you approach a weakness and build up the courage to keep reworking and readjusting your pathway to success.

Thomas gave the example of requiring a problem-solving related project every year in high school and having the problem being school-focused to encourage civic engagement. An experiential class like that has the potential to make you feel unstoppable in a pursuit to fail, learn, and collaborate with others.

In turn, during my junior year, I joined a college healthcare theatre class and started to pitch more often. In healthcare theatre, students who are interested in the medical field become their patients through simulated case studies, while practicing nursing students exercise their classroom knowledge in real time. This way I could become comfortable with interpersonal feedback and attention to growth. By interweaving my desire to become more proficient in public speaking and learn more about nursing, I was able to engage my mind in refining a new skill and connecting deeper with an innovative community.

As a simulated patient, I once experienced Emergency Room chaos in a way I never had before in an actual hospital. There were four nursing students in the room and my character, Jordan Rivera, was recovering from a post-surgical appendectomy (removal of an appendix). They checked my vitals (blood pressure, temperature, breathing, pulse) and minimally asked about my life outside of the operating table. After taking fake medication for Jordan's pain, I became a body on a bed. The vital sign monitor started going off like crazy.

Sitting there in only a hospital gown and under (fake) post-anesthesia, I was terrified. What was going on? Why was that noise repeatedly alarming the frantic nurses? They seemed to have forgotten that Jordan existed and as a patient Jordan felt neglected and alone.

The scenario continued to play out until it ended. An assistant came in and gave me a clipboard to begin giving feedback on how the team performed.

When the instructor declared the simulation over, the students looked calm.

What?!

Why?

Because they knew that even though they had "failed," the constructive feedback would help them to tweak what went wrong and continue to help them get the practice right until it came time for them to go out and be nurses, for real.

With this method, they were able to become familiar with deconstructing a situation and working toward making it more efficient the next time and the next time, so their real patients would never experience what I (Jordan) went through again.

**

Some experts claim it's better to see failure as an experiment as opposed to a restrictive destination. Think of it like this, at some point in your education journey, you were likely forced into or happily endured a school science project. There, you learned the basics of the scientific method—the most practical advice from this field that applies to any field whether you become a scientist or not.

We can use the scientific method in any approach toward success and effective problem-solving. Looking at failure as something malleable and retestable helps build confidence in yourself and makes the next iterations much better than your initial one.

Sara Blakely, founder of Spanx, said that her history of being comfortable with failure led her to build a business from scratch, even though she had no experience.[25] This technique applies in fashion, business, human resources, and anywhere else failure can occur.

---

25 Cooper, Belle Beth. "The Science Of Failure: Why Highly Successful People Crave Mistakes." Resources.

You must be willing to see your downfalls as opportunities to build up your character, fail tolerance, and personal credibility.

When you are comfortable with the idea that failure isn't negative and can be turned into a cherished lifelong lesson, then you can truly embrace what I summed up my high school experience as: "no bad days."

Barbara Corcoran, an investor from the hit show *Shark Tank*, gave a TEDx talk about rethinking failure.[26] She wasn't always at the top of her game, but she got there because her "best successes all come on the heels of failure."[27] Even the most well-established entrepreneurs understand the value of taking failure for all it's worth.

At the end of the day, the grades you get in high school will never be asked of you for a job interview post-graduation. What matters instead are the traits you pick up; humility, discipline, and tolerance from failure will help you on your track to becoming your best self.

If you take a moment to step back and look at your current successes, no matter how big or how small, there was a person or feeling or circumstance that propelled you there *after you faced adversity.*

So now what?

---

26 Singju, Pangambam. "Barbara Corcoran: Rethinking Failure At Tedx-BarnardCollege (Transcript)." The Singju Post.

27 Ibid

Take these tips to embrace failure and re-identify your intentions toward academic and extracurricular success:

1. **Create a failure statement.** Make your own mantra for recitation after a failure to remind you that you can learn from it as opposed to wallowing in it.
   a. You can even borrow Barbara's! "My best successes all come on the heels of failure. My best successes all come on the heels of failure. My best successes all come on the heels of failure." Recognize the power of the self-fulfilling prophecy.

2. **Fail in PUBLIC!** I cannot stress the importance of letting others see your failure. Once you get past the idea that failure is shameful, you can firmly reinforce the practice of accepting the situation. Also, by publicly announcing your weaknesses, you are redefining "downfalls" and turning them into "uplifts."
   a. You can reach out to someone who has gone through a similar situation; they may have helpful advice for gathering all the best tips from it. You will begin to see yourself as an unabashed traveler on the pursuit of fully equipped success. Others will feed off your courage as well!

3. **Practice the Scientific Method and take bigger risks.** I know you expected me to give you a detailed account on how to get an A, but the truth is, your grades are completely relative. The short answer is to pay attention, sit still, and keep your eyes glued to the teacher. The genuine answer is to utilize the process of reiteration to create a scoring system that values your full understanding and

application of school subjects, rather that your ability to guess.

    a. Then, using that process, you will find taking big, personal risks outside of your comfort zone—like a doing pitch competition or performing in a theater class or joining youth advocacy initiatives—generates more enjoyment and social impact than your grades ever will.

When you break away from the idea failure equates to a loss, you can begin to value the practical skills school is supposed to teach you. You will do what I call turning failure into fortitude.

TAKEAWAYS & LESSONS:

- With the recognition of your faults, you will pave a much clearer path to your future—one that is not dependent on a number or average.
- Use the knowledge you are more than a grade; with that, you can work toward creating independent paths of learning.

CALL TO ACTION

I challenge you to fail fast and in public. Then tweak your method toward the problem you are trying to solve in order to reach your definition of success.

CHAPTER 7

HACK HOMEWORK: CREATING INDEPENDENT STUDIES

"Do your homework and know your facts but remember it's passion that persuades."

— H. JACKSON BROWN, JR.

Students across the United States mindlessly spend hours in a stone-cold building. Some end up leaving in a state like the rigid, unoriginal, and bleak place. In most cases, you do have the desire to learn, but because of the infinite list of curriculum requirements, you may never dig deeper into the subject material.

In order to redesign the purpose of school to revolutionize and embody the elements of a twenty-first century learner, you need three things: independence, determination, and exposure.

School is supposed to represent a haven for the exhibition of skills, talents, and creativity. The current system, however, inhibits these key elements.

As a student, I strive to acquire a strong sense of independence in my daily routine. Independence as in living my life as I see fit, without any restrictions or handholding. When I was younger, I started to recognize the lack of intuition in my daily routine. I would wake up with my siblings at 6 a.m., be in my first class before 8 a.m. and be on the road back home before 3 p.m.

The numbers six, eight, and three represented my pie chart of freedom and how much sooner I had until I could return home to something more fulfilling.

That is not to say that I didn't enjoy school, but there were some days where I questioned the practical application of complex fractions and amoebas in the real world. This divide between what seemed real and what was rote confused and concerned me the most when I started high school.

If everything I was learning had a purpose, why not clue me in on what that exact purpose is?

From this question stemmed my quest for what a great education was and how to obtain it in the two years I had left. The time I spent in school was beyond my power—an uncontrollable clock. The long hand spun rapidly as I struggled to grasp kinetics in AP Chemistry or the subjunctive tense in Spanish 3. I couldn't gauge how long it would take for my mind to understand objectives; the time I spent frustrated usually outweighed the time I spent enjoying the material. For English, in a span of five to fifteen minutes I could cram twenty vocabulary words and still manage to forget them all in the next two hours.

The cycle of memorization was king to the application of the concepts and terms I would be continuously tested on for the next nine months.

Education pioneer Sir Kenneth Robinson summarized this problem best in his 2010 TED Talk. According to Robinson, what schools are encouraged to do is to find out what kids can do across a very narrow spectrum of achievement.[28]

Even if I can memorize twenty words in fifteen minutes, what does that say about my ability to effectively communicate my ideas to a group?

Knowing a random set of words without applying and using them in my life often got lost in my pursuit of an A. In an hour and a half, I had taken notes about a topic I would forget over a thirty-minute lunch and attempt to cram twelve hours before the closing exam.

**

There are pros and cons to mindless memorization. Think about it like this:

---

28 Robinson, Ken. "Bring On The Learning Revolution!" TED video, 17:51. Posted February 2010.

You're watching a 3v3 basketball game and everyone you know—aunts, uncles, teachers, and parents—are cheering for team TL. But you'd like to root for team FL on the DU. (Team TL stands for Temporary Learning. Team FL on the DU stands for Forever Learning on the Deeper Understanding.)

Who will be more prepared to win the game?

Leaning heavily on memorizing facts and equations and literary characters often interferes with deeper learning. Much of the content we try to shove into our brains is lost when done this way. However, with deeper learning, we can learn how to relate the knowledge to other areas of our lives and effectively use it in a variety of situations.

The Business Growth Leader at Thinkster Math, Rupa Gurumurthy, reported that "according to cognitive scientists, each time the brain is given new information, it has to make a decision: is this information relevant and worth remembering? If so, it will make the effort to store the information in its long-term memory. If not, the likelihood of being able to efficiently 'transfer' the knowledge is much lower."[29] When deciding whether to make the lay-up or pass the ball, rote memorization drops it.

How does rote memorization prepare us for other things?

If you have reviewed a concept over and over, as opposed to using it only once, you are practicing what Oakland

---

29 Gurumurthy, Rupa and Kendra Straley, et al. "Rote Memorization Vs. Critical Thinking: How Online Math Tutors Help." Thinkster Math.

math teacher Ben Orlin calls repeated use. By intentionally using the facts in your life, they may become beneficial. The important idea though is using the already-known facts as building blocks for new knowledge.[30] This technique relies on connections and associations.

Orlin says, "It's a mistake to downplay factual knowledge, as if students could learn to reason critically without any information to reason about. But memorization's opponents are right: Memorized knowledge isn't half as useful as knowledge that's actually understood."[31]

Now, of course, memory is good for recalling your best friend's phone number or an emergency contact, but the benefits of memorization are essentially non-existent and its consequences can be harmful.

** **

Time contributes heavily to our ability to generate interest in the subject material. When we spend less time on understanding, our motive for learning often gets blended into the unfortunate path of what Robinson points out as "a culture of compliance. Our children and teachers are encouraged to follow routine algorithms rather than to excite that power of imagination and curiosity."[32] This prospect of hammering away on topics causes students to devalue the creative

---

30 Orlin, Ben. 2013. "When Memorization Gets In The Way Of Learning." *The Atlantic.*

31 Ibid.

32 Robinson, Ken. "Bring On The Learning Revolution!" TED video, 17:51. Posted February 2010.

process and focus on having numbers above nine or ten in their toolbox.

After all, if the only thing required for success is following a list of requirements, then branching out of one's interests is futile and meaningless.

"If my test scores are higher than the person next to me, then that must mean I have more value than they have and ever will."

This flawed mindset disregards the reality that every student has a vast range of abilities. Just because you may not perfectly show it academically doesn't mean your capabilities cannot shine in another way.

I believe the most powerful students are the ones who take charge of their learning both outside and inside of the classroom. They find ways to implement opportunity into their school day and take their teachers along.

**

The way I see it, anyone can be creative and independent.

Absolutely anyone.

It's what you pursue with your resources that will enable you to hack homework, high school, and the highway. Okay, not that last one. That's a skill you'll have to master in Driver's Ed.

One thing I could never understand about school is how we spend years practicing our writing skills, which are important, but little to no time on our speaking techniques.

I know there are other factors to work on building, such as social identity and presence in front of a crowd, but speaking to people or communicating ideas to a large group is one of the most disregarded gifts that school fails to get across to its students.

To compensate for not having audio as an option on an assignment, you can request to submit a video recording, animated short film, or audio file. Or you could start a podcast instead of doing written book reviews!

You need to become comfortable with the sound of your own voice so you can build up confidence to convey your ideas passionately and creatively. You can practice this by reading books aloud, creating speeches, starting a YouTube channel, a podcast, or radio show.

If your teachers are not on board with submitting an assignment in a different format, try explaining to them how you plan to go about this process and how it can better aid your learning.

This micro-fix may well be the first step in convincing your teachers you'd like to do things differently to complement your creative thought process and thinking skills.

**

Independent models of learning have been called the "flipped-model" of education, but why?

In college, the place where most high school students spend countless hours to prepare for, the professors assign work, you interpret it in your own way, and then you bring those ideas to the classroom. In a later chapter, you will hear about a college student named Morgan Rollins who transformed what education meant to her. In order to do that, she asked her administrators if she could create her own prosthetic class to count as a high school course. She had a teacher as an advisor, designed her own lesson plans, and ended up building a life-changing prosthetic leg.

Given our unique ways of understanding information, how cool would it be if your high school allowed you to make your own course? What's stopping you from asking?

You can also discover more about your desire to learn a new topic when you can solve problems without a recycled template or script. Create a script of your own!

Kimani Calliste, a New York creative and celebrity photographer, wishes high school had prepared him for the social aspects of the workforce.

He has had the opportunity to work with different high-class media companies and freelance jobs for community nonprofits. I met him through GripTape, an organization that strives to allow students to have complete decision-making power over their learning with adults as their guides—not their instructors. His own school environment did not encourage design-thinking or the pursuit of projects outside of the curriculum.

However, he chose to defy the restrictive mold and take his artistic skills to a higher level.

He wanted to work on ideas for which he would keep himself accountable. For example, he started his own photography business, created a club, and practiced screen-writing frequently.

"Perhaps, too frequently," he confesses.

Kimani admits he didn't find interest in his math classes and instead chose to create scripts out of the ongoing ideas in his head. He wasn't an A+ student and didn't have a phenomenal GPA, but he steadfastly followed his interests in his own unique way.

"I learned more from starting a business than I did in my traditional business class," he said.

This is where an independent study course could have benefited him instead.

Sometimes building an independent study means dedicating yourself to an endeavor that takes place outside of school or in small pockets of free time. Kimani clues that majors should start being set from high schools to streamline the possibilities. Majors in college can be translated as independent studies in your high school and at home.

I do believe our academics are important, but at the expense of leaving out or tossing aside our true potentials, ways of understanding, or desires to dig deeper…I am not a fan.

Kimani knew he struggled with his interest in STEM and chose to master his art. If his high school had created pathways like majors in his education, he could have combined his love for photography with other subjects in his curriculum.

According to Youth Truth, a national education non-profit that surveys youth, only forty-six percent of high school students feel what they're learning in class helps them outside of school.[33]

Over half of students in that survey aren't finding value in the material being taught beyond the classroom. Just as there are "undecided" majors in college, we could start to have those kinds of options for high school students as well. They would have the choice to declare a major by sophomore year or stay undecided until graduation. The undecided track could mirror traditional high school with a laundry list of general requirements and foundational knowledge.

Would you go in undecided? It is certainly something to consider.

**

If you're an avid fan of homework, or merely tolerate it, look closer at the statistics.

---

33   "Student Engagement - Youthtruth." 2019. Youthtruth.

Stanford researchers found in a study that "allocating the majority of your time to homework means sacrificing your independence toward developing your talents and skills. Students in the study said they were more likely to forgo activities, stop seeing friends or family, and not participate in hobbies."[34]

Dr. Denise Pope, PhD, is a senior lecturer at Stanford's School of Education and coauthored the study. She highlighted that students can acquire skills even when less homework is assigned. She told *Monitor on Psychology* a story about "one teacher she worked with who taught Advanced Placement Biology and experimented by dramatically cutting down homework assignments. First the teacher cut homework by a third, and then cut the assignments in half. The students' test scores didn't change."[35]

Imagine creating your own homework assignments and having the chance to focus on areas that need the most work.

According to the U.S. News and World Report, a "survey of 1,000 K-12 teachers found, among other things, that high school teachers on average assign about 3.5 hours of homework each week. For high school students who typically have five classes with different teachers, that could mean as much as 17.5 hours each week."[36] Now I don't know about your

---

34 Levy, Sandra and Dr. Karen Gill. "Is Too Much Homework Bad for Kids' Health?" Healthline.

35 Ibid

36 Bidwell, Allie. "Students Spend More Time on Homework but Teachers Say It's Worth It." *U.S. News and World Report,* February 27, 2014.

schedule, but the lowest number of classes I've had in a school year was definitely higher than five.

Homework, without a doubt, is essential. That said, the amount of work students currently receive **often goes beyond their actual understanding** of the topic and lessens the chance of it being enjoyable to learn.

When you're swamped with assignments, it's hard to concentrate on honing your interest.

In my experience, I have learned best from turning the rigid objectives into unstructured "subjectives" (personalized learning points) and connecting concepts to elements of my real life. When you have the academic freedom to step beyond the limited scope of mandated curriculum, genuine learning takes place.

TAKEAWAYS & LESSONS:
- The independence to take charge of personal learning endeavors is critical for life in grade school and in careers.
- Imagine being in an art class with half of the portrait already painted for you, then being told to paint something specific which you cannot visualize for yourself.
  - We cannot cultivate creativity from completed pieces and parts of an idea. Educators must allow us to wander off the traditional path of learning and find out what makes us want to learn more.
- The start of innovation is when students feel more compelled to enhance their individual projects. With a little bit of requested assistance and a plethora of support for

what we come up with, the classroom can turn into a safe haven for creative ideas to come to life.

- There is no finite end to learning and the idea that Grade 12 is where it ends is beyond false.
- Students who go through the experiential process of information are more likely to interpret the complexities of core topics and apply them to the real world. The way most people end up in their respective fields is through exposure to ideas they had not previously considered.

If you could scale to size the power of active learning, the results would be tremendous. Education can be a lot more effective when the right strategies are being utilized. Students who have these three traits—independence, determination, and exposure—often demonstrate their ability to think uniquely instead of with unoriginal and recycled methods.

There are many strategies you can take toward "flipped" learning and when you look at the results you will start to really feel, dare I say, excited. Once you have conquered the classroom, you can begin to retrain the way you think about education.

CALL TO ACTION
I challenge you to create an independent study of choice on a topic you've never learned about, like supply-chain, Bitcoin, poetry, electronics, fashion, world history, photography, and financial literacy. Then, teach what you've discovered to someone else who doesn't know much about the topic.

PART 2

HOW TO RETRAIN YOUR MIND

CHAPTER 8

PUBLIC (SCHOOL) ENEMY NUMBER ONE...TEACHERS?

———

"The art of teaching is the art of assisting discovery."
— MARK VAN DOREN

"Do I not destroy my enemies when I make them my friends?"
— ABRAHAM LINCOLN

Since the first day of kindergarten, our teachers have been portrayed as our second parents whose responsibilities were to take care of their children at various points of the day. Maybe you've seen a teacher as an obstacle or bridge to something you want. Either way, these "second parents" play a huge role in who we are and in how we treat ourselves, our ideas, and our minds.

From that first interaction, we learn to see them as big, older people. We learn to see them as leaders and pioneers of their fields. We learn to see them as *human beings.*

I also learned to see them as enemies. How?

Well, there was the way I thought that their personal dislike or appreciation of me could affect my grade in the class, or how my siblings' past performances and behaviors could benefit or destroy my relationship with them.

I remember classes where I wouldn't call a teacher out on their mistakes for fear of losing my precious position in their good graces.

Teachers have a long laundry list of actions they must take in ensuring all their students receive the best they can give. Seeing a teacher as an enemy feels unfair, inappropriate even.

Although they receive a paycheck (not a hefty one), they likely did not go into the field with money as their main priority. Plus, there is a surplus of bad anything—bad doctors, bad lawyers, and bad accountants; the list goes on. However, it only seems that way because they are either new to the game or are still trying to mentally map how to fit and meet everyone's needs.

Your teachers won't always agree to what you suggest or think. They are the ones, after all, who went to school to study their field. Just like an argument with your parents, there are a few topics with your teachers you simply cannot win.

In those moments, when you feel like both of your parents are against you, what do you do?

What if your ideas don't matter to them or it seems like they don't care about what the middle child thinks?

I used to blame my teachers for anything when it went wrong. The way I proceeded to do so wasn't obnoxious; I felt like I was actively facing opposition when I expressed an idea and didn't receive any feedback or support.

When examining the many flaws of this age-old education system, I realized almost everything was indeed outdated and did not meet the needs of the new tech-savvy, entrepreneurial generation.

So, whose fault was it? Who was the enemy from within restricting real change from taking off?

I had a full circle understanding of who was to blame during my junior year.

All my past experiences set up expectations for new teachers and my current knowledge built biases of how to distinguish a good teacher versus an intentional enemy.

In middle school, the entire eighth grade team of teachers filled my year with creativity and curiosity. They went above and beyond to create interesting lectures (at least to me) and made sure project-based learning was a key part of our environment. I saw my science, social studies, English, math, and art teachers as respectable allies. From studying earth facts and the Boston Massacre to designing book diaries and 3D wall art, I grew as a perspective listener and introspective storyteller.

If middle school were a big basketball game, I had all the right players on my team. I walked away from that school year with only one number on my report card—one hundred.

What? That's crazy. I really don't believe you.

Yes! And I'm not the only one. Several new techniques in project-based learning are showing early success. The George Lucas Education Foundation found a recent collaborative study conducted by the University of Michigan and Michigan State University which suggests the implementation of project-based learning (PBL) correlated positively with student achievement, especially in high-poverty environments.[37]

The economic surroundings in Wilmington, Delaware (dubbed Murder Town in 2014, due to the large number of black youth being killed every year[38]) certainly affected the attitude toward learning in my school. I had classmates whose friends died from constant gun violence, so coming to a place that welcomed their minds to think creatively shaped the culture of our classes. It also encouraged me to ask questions and provide support as a student who lived half an hour away from all the madness.

---

37 Duke, Nell K. and Anne-Lise Halvorsen. "New Study Shows The Impact Of PBL On Student Achievement." Edutopia.

38 Jones, Abigail. "Murder Town USA (aka Wilmington, Delaware)." *Newsweek,* December 9, 2014.

Additional studies comparing learning outcomes for students taught with project-based learning versus traditional instruction show that when implemented well, PBL **increases long-term retention** of content, helps students perform as well as or better than traditional learners in high-stakes tests, **improves problem-solving and collaboration skills**, and **improves students' attitudes** towards learning.[39]

I'm not including this story to have a subtle flex on Chapter 6; I loved going the extra mile in every single class. It felt like I had purpose and value in the content being presented to me. In hindsight, I saw those teachers as great mentors, giving me daily conversation while standing up in front of a room of other listeners.

When we were learning about The Renaissance Period in English class, I was assigned the topic of Colonial Weddings.

Presentation day rolled around and when I stood up there, the feeling of being a certified wedding planner washed over me—I forgot I was just an eighth grade English student. My poster board featured the magic of felt with sharpie, intricate red, trimmed flowers, jumbo glass gems, and blurbs of text.

I wanted my classmates and teacher to feel like I was their confidant, their BFF, *their certified wedding planner*, who was going to make sure that their special day turned out spectacular.

---

39 Teach & Kids Learn (TKL). "Does Project-Based Learning Increase Student Learning? What Does Research Say?"

But it wasn't always like this.

I have had my fair share of 'teachers-who-will-not-be-mentioned' who still pushed me to do my best work. They weren't particularly rude or disrespectful, I just never found myself running to them for advice outside of class.

When my high school journey started, social studies wasn't as fun, and like I said, English became a class about receiving information instead of searching for it myself. Math honestly roundhouse kicked me in the stomach in terms of how frustrating it was to have to take geometry for the second time.

Needless to say, things were very different. More specifically, I met the opponent's weapon: busywork. The transition in the increase of assignments and the decrease in the amount of dedicated attention made me forget the value of deep understanding.

English started off with my overly annotated summer reading, *The Color of Water: A Black Man's Tribute to His White Mother* by James McBride, and the disheartening feeling that it had to be one of my "quiet-classes."

*Regular classes were periods where I felt particularly engaged, due to the teacher's style of lecturing and the level of student involvement. However, **quiet classes** were the periods where I sat and listened to the lessons bounce from the teacher's mouth and onto my blank sheet of notes. I didn't feel engaged with the material or have the desire to connect with it beyond the homework assignments.*

The problem stemmed from the loss of project-based learning and genuine concern for how differently my peers and I learned. I loved writing in the eighth grade; in high school it turned into yet another task on my never-ending to-do list.

**

Fast-forward to the end of sophomore year. Project-based learning became my superpower through out-of-school programs like Dual School and GripTape.

At the onset of my junior year, I embarked on a new journey. I wanted to start a program at my high school which encouraged my peers and me to engage in the practice of peer-mentoring, learning public speaking skills, and networking with the community. In order to proceed with my idea, I needed a club adviser to guide us as the year went along.

I decided to choose my freshmen year English teacher to join me in my goal to spearhead a school-wide lean toward fostering leadership potential.

But why her? Isn't that the same teacher who taught one of my freshmen "quiet-classes?"

The truth was, I admired her ambition in executing her goals in a timely fashion. I wanted to learn more about how to do the same. With her skills—management and creative thinking—I knew her guidance would be pivotal in making sure the first year went smoothly.

She said yes, thankfully, and ended up being the adviser for the new program and a club I had been chosen as president for at the end of tenth grade.

Here's why teachers are **NOT** the enemy, even though at the beginning it might seem to be the case.

As I worked directly with her on something I was passionate about, I realized she had her own life to navigate as well.

With both groups, the Student Leadership Initiative Program and the UNICEF (United Nations International Children's Emergency Fund) club, she kindly opened her classroom as the space to grow community, hone ideas, discuss politics and international affairs, mentor underclassmen, run design sessions, collect over 1,000 books for a children's drive, and plan for a leadership panel. And not once did she complain about it.

Just kidding. She's human too. Plus, have you ever tried to organize a community event in less than two months without pulling your hair out?

We had plenty of moments of frustration, growth, learning, and conversation that went beyond the surface of my original perception of her. I knew if I could go back in time, I would urge my freshman self to see my teachers as mentors who had years of experience and wisdom in their toolboxes ready to equip the next generations with the tools needed for thoughtful impact.

This English teacher of mine started off as just that—an English teacher.

However, when I reached out to her about two projects, I knew would be more successful with her help, and realized she had extensive responsibilities as a mother, teacher, mentor, and now, friend.

**

Bryce Fender, founder of WilmInvest, a real-estate investment startup, Dual School mentor, and University of Delaware graduate, talked about the difference between feeling like you are learning and feeling like you are a puppet. This comparison in identity roles will build or break your relationship with a teacher.

However, for there to be motion in a student's dreams or ideas, we need to have the freedom to experience it. Fender stresses it is better to "empower kids to be passionate about their own problems" rather than a textbook problem which students continue to solve repeatedly.

Think about when you first experienced the weather as a kid. For example, if someone told me about snow falling on the ground, I would run to the window to experience it myself. As American gardener Elizabeth Lawrence said, "Everyone must take time to sit and watch the leaves turn."

You must go out and face those changes by yourself, so when you really are on your own, you would've had the time to ask how to approach it from a different angle and fix it with that new view.

Luckily, like the changes of color in leaves, the relationships you have with your teachers can also change.

Another reason why teachers are not the enemy is that they are only one part of the American education system.

As the writers from the Educators Room advocate "The ultimate goal of schools is to help students become productive citizens in society. By that reasoning, there should be multiple steps taken to support teachers, since they have the most direct contact with students of anyone else in a school. When teachers feel supported, students benefit. When students benefit from schools, society benefits as a whole. Isn't that what we all want anyway?"[40]

This is exactly what I wanted then and what I want now for the school system.

Seeing our teachers as allies will enable the start of difficult conversations that have to do with the way they are poorly treated. "Retraining" your mind towards your teachers begins with you changing the narrative. They are vital characters, not enemies, in your story.

---

40   The Educator's Room. "How Students Lose When Teachers Become The Enemy."

According to researchers from *Frontiers in Psychology*, teachers' relationship experiences with students are an important daily source of teacher emotion and cognition, potentially affecting a teacher's well-being.[41] Your enemy certainly wouldn't care much about you or make the effort to build a good relationship.

Communication is a two-way street and your collaboration needs to be mutual. So how can you still think they are the enemy?

The next time your relationships with your teachers aren't working out smoothly:

- Consider making a portfolio of your ideas and projects and set up a meeting to get to know them.
- Talk to your teachers about things that are not strictly school related.
- Learn about them and their interests as they'll usually try to do the same for you.
- Find out what they have a passion for. If your passions align, it'll make for great conversation! If you have different passions, you can learn more about how they approach problem-solving.
- Remember you only have nine months to get to know them as an asset to your success as opposed to a boulder in your path.

---

41   Milatz, Anne, Marko Lüftenegger, and Barbara Schober. "Teachers' Relationship Closeness With Students As A Resource For Teacher Wellbeing: A Response Surface Analytical Approach." *Frontiers In Psychology* 6 (2015): 1949.

Becoming a teacher is a huge and impactful choice that alters the way entire communities respond to the world.

I used to view teachers who I didn't particularly form a bond with as bystanders in my process of learning, but when you take intentional steps to include them in the conversation you'll realize they have been by your side, listening and observing, the whole time.

TAKEAWAYS & LESSONS:
- Teachers are not the enemy. When you take the time to get to know them on a personal level, you might be surprised by what you find.
- Learning is much more engaging if it's like talking to one of your friends. Not only that, the process is easier when you feel comfortable asking questions about confusing material you didn't immediately understand.
- Help your teachers! If you have a personal project they could assist you with, don't be afraid to ask, ask, ask! There's a good chance they'll help you get closer to achieving a milestone in some way, either directly or by connecting you with another person who can help.
- Don't be a puppet when it comes to your learning, repeating the words in your notes as they appear on the slides. Make the curriculum align with your interests.

CALL TO ACTION
I challenge you to resolve any and all problems you had with teachers from your past years of school. Find a way to reach common ground about issues you dealt with when you were with them or are currently dealing with in your life.

CHAPTER 9

CURRICULUM WARS: WHO IS RESPONSIBLE FOR THE DAMAGE?

———

"Education is not just about going to school and getting a degree. It's about widening your knowledge and absorbing the truth about life."

— SHAKUNTALA DEVI

"There is no end to education. It is not that you read a book, pass an examination, and finish with education. The whole of life, from the moment you are born to the moment you die, is a process of learning."

— JIDDU KRISHNAMURTI

We don't go to school to learn. We attend school and we're taught. We go to regurgitate answers, not to ask questions.

Many students don't subscribe to the three sentences above, but our current model of education does.

School's purpose, in the shortest of phrases, is to captivate the attention of young learners to ponder more on the world as they know it.

However, our curriculum does not achieve this daring sentence.

It makes me wonder: is there a way to fix it?

Right now, there is a war between who has the authority to change the curriculum or decide whether it should change at all.

**

Think about it. The fact that fewer than thirty-five percent of Americans can name every state in four minutes is absurd.[42] And yet, the importance of American civics and geography is not stressed as much as it should be. The voting process, where we live, how our government works, and our rights, in my experience, are all topics covered in a quick swoop that is freshmen year and then as an option in AP Government by the time we're ready to graduate.

There is no doubt that this information battle affects students in America, but it also brings up the question of how

---

42   Stopera, Dave. "Less Than 35% Of Americans Can Name Every State In 4 Minutes, Can You?" Buzzfeed, February 27, 2019.

we interact with global politics and think outside ourselves, when we don't even know where our own places are located.

I took the states quiz on Sporcle, the world's largest trivia quiz website, trying to visually name and correctly identify the states. I got forty-one of the fifty states in around eight minutes.

I don't know how I would have performed with only four.

I challenge you to do the same, whether it's in this book with the map provided, online, or by listing them on a blank sheet of paper with a timer. The frustration I felt from forgetting Pennsylvania, Oklahoma, the Virginias, Connecticut, Mississippi, and Iowa (the others I wasn't too surprised: Oregon and Montana) is hard to describe.

I felt stupid not knowing all fifty states we reference in the Pledge at the start of every school morning. The information was myopic, or not explicitly relevant to our lives, after the fifth grade!

"I PLEDGE ALLEGIANCE TO THE FLAG OF *THE UNITED STATES OF AMERICA*, AND TO THE REPUBLIC FOR WHICH IT STANDS, ONE NATION UNDER GOD, INDIVISIBLE, WITH LIBERTY AND JUSTICE FOR ALL."

So, what does not remembering all the states or being taught about governmental policy beyond the three branches of government say about the curriculum? Who is responsible for this atrocity?

Our government and political studies are key to our identities as citizens and voters. There are many other subjects we should study closer and include in the curriculum, but they never seem to make it to the requirements list.

Among those are American Sign Language, International Relations, Financial Literacy, Public Speaking 101, Professionalism Online, Survival Skills, Nutrition, Mindfulness, Anthropology, Sustainable Living, and of course, independent studies.[43]

**

We walk into class, battle-ready, armed with our sharpened number two pencils, 200+ page textbooks, and sleep-deprived bodies—anxious for the events of the school day.

---

43   Clayton, Sarah. "These Are The Subjects That Should ACTUALLY Be Taught In Secondary Schools."

Every moment moves like an animation; frame by frame we watch the pieces come together without a say or reaction to the progression of the moment. We watch, we wait, and we walk, only to go through the same drill in the morning. Eyes closed, feet flat, and minds off, consciously vacuuming in intel that cannot categorize itself efficiently.

War is a very subjective topic.

We learn about wars throughout history, beefs between friend groups, and even through the examination of issues in the political sphere. Each story has a basic structure with heroes and villains and their sidekicks and accomplices. However, when talking about the element of control in the classroom who plays what role?

In the last chapter, we clarified that teachers are not the enemy. Rather, they are our allies.

I want to show you the trajectory of change in our current curriculum and what other alternatives schools need to take in order to become a more informed and informing environment.

This exaggerated war scene makes me wonder how often we've been placed in a situation to which control was withheld and reserved for a commander (likely an adult) in power. School is at the forefront of our existence; from the onset of pre-school to the anticipated decision day in May which leads us to our next primary source of attention.

Having a life outside of school is seen as abnormal in some cases because of the long hours we spend completing tasks centered around the learning that happens in the building.

This same scenario happens in our classrooms, particularly when it comes to our curriculum. We are loaded up with backpacks full of items which have no personalized purpose and are told to keep fighting—age group by age group, the war will slowly end.

But if the end of this war is graduation, why are we walking into battle practically blindfolded and told the battle we experienced will help us in the future?

In terms of school, we have math, English, science, social studies, and maybe an additional elective course. The dictionary defines elective as "a course of study chosen by the student rather than compulsory." However, most of those classes must fill the requirements to graduate.

When we are withheld choice in our education, it is hard to see the "bigger picture" of guaranteed success or the victory in a mandatory war.

We need to redefine learning objectives specifically in high school because the war on learning has continued to exclude its most dedicated soldiers—students. After all, what's the point of learning things we will forget two days later? One week? One year? Our entire lives?

The war on learning refers to the lack of choice students have in recreating the curriculum due to its lack of engagement.

Tony Miller, a writer for the U.S. Department of Education, said that "every year, over 1.2 million students drop out of high school in the United States alone. That's a student every 26 seconds – or 7,000 a day."[44]

Imagine how many lives would change if our curriculum reflected the interests of our current student body. If businesses and companies had the same limitations of the high school curriculum in terms of change and control, our economy wouldn't look so good. Innovation means allowing change to revolutionize an idea as it ages. Our system is old and desperately needs an update. As Miller pointed out, the result of halting innovation has not been positive.[45]

Businesses cannot thrive without happy customers because those same customers drive the market as they participate in it.

For years, we have been unhappy with the shortcomings of high school and it's time for much-needed change.

We've established there is damage from years of disregard, but we need to be the ones to say, "I am tired of mindlessly searching for drive in subjects that motivate me to stay seated." Our education must lift off!

---

44   Do Something. "11 Facts About High School Dropout Rates."
45   Ibid.

**

Innovation is incredibly important for driving change. Students who don't have a say, do not have a future.

Now, how do we combat this?

A. J. Juliani, acclaimed author of the books *Empower, Intentional Innovation,* and *Launch,* wrote about this in an eduTopia article about time. "We spend 14,256 hours in school between kindergarten and graduation. If we can't find a time for students to have some choice in their learning, then what are we doing with all those hours?"[46]

> *One way to teach autonomy in education is the concept of 20% Time. It is when teachers allow their students twenty percent of class time, or one hour per week, to work on and explore topics of their choice.*

How have lawmakers continued to let students spend almost 15,000 hours without a single choice? Riddle me that!

"Instead of answering a multiple-choice test on *The Great Gatsby,* **why can't my daughter have the opportunity to write, collaborate, sing and produce a song that explains in detail the major themes of the story?** Through 20% Time, we give our students a voice in their own learning and allow them to go into depth in subjects that we may skim over in our curriculum."[47] Juliani brings up an interesting idea I urge

---

46 Juliani, A.J. "The 20% Project (Like Google) In My Class."
47 Ibid

you to take part in. By standing up to traditional education ideals, we can bring in 20% Time as the gradual change agent for making education more personalized and experiential.

What would you do with 20% Time? Juliani highlights, "The idea for 20% Time in schools comes from Google's own 20% policy, where employees are given twenty percent of their time to work and innovate on something else besides their current project."[48]

Now how about that?

Working hard on a project you are passionate about for twenty percent of your day will give you the same one hundred percent satisfaction Google employees likely enjoy.

We don't have to hold back from engaging in the 20% Time; on our own time, we can be the members who are both making an impact and happy with their progression in life.

Adding this method to the curriculum would completely revolutionize school. Just take twenty percent of your day and dedicate it to a creative work or ongoing solution. When you can find enjoyment in your studies, school transforms from building and into a catalytic center for imagination. Imagine labeling your school with that phrase.

What will it take?

I spoke with one of my State Senators to find out.

---

48 Ibid

**

Senator Elizabeth "Tizzy" Lockman sees school itself as a great space for social education.

She upholds the idea of "explicit teaching, of civics, social justice, and all that stuff gets a short strip, because when you have a great social studies teacher, it's just transformative. How cool would it be to have a former legislator, be your kid's social studies teacher?"

"What we need to do is stop prescribing curriculum and start pushing a framework within which we have to allow educators to be professionals and figure out the best way to deliver to students and get students on board with that content, which I think will vary depending on the students."

Schools must be driven by context rather than content.

I mean, imagine having a classroom of thirty kids and having to figure out how to know the strengths and weaknesses of every child—that is an art, not a science."
— SENATOR TIZZY LOCKMAN

Lockman brings up a great point about context. Every single student in the world, no matter what school you go to and which country you reside in, is facing a different academic battle and need that does not always parallel with the needs of other students in their respective countries.

Collectively, we are so much more than obedient kids who don't have voices of our own to contribute to the conversation.

Here's how to lift off and find beauty in the rubble:

- Encourage your teachers to take on 20% Time into their lesson plans.
- Pursue with confidence on your path to learning to learn, rather than learning to score.
- Be captivated by the learning process and the many ways you can branch out of the one-size-fits-all curriculum.

Seeing the problem with the curriculum from a pessimistic standpoint will not help in redesigning it. Even though, in times past, this method of ignoring student concerns and shielding us from the situation might have made the process go faster, potential speed is no longer something that educators should continue to bank on.

By taking charge of what exactly is going on behind the scenes, we can retrain our minds to prepare to be career-ready and open to representation conversations.

TAKEAWAYS & LESSONS:
- Civics and Geography are very important. You should know your fifty states. If you don't live in America, knowing the areas surrounding you is equally as important.

As an American high school student, I felt the need to highlight this point, but it doesn't redefine the fact we should all know where we are in relation to *what.*

- The war on curriculum has been going on for many, many, many years now. It is up to our generation to break the cycle of repetition and start learning about topics that are relevant.
- Have these kinds of conversations with your friends about how you would recreate the high school curriculum. Think about ways to create solutions you can present to teachers and administrators.
- Integrate A. J. Juliani's 20% Time into your everyday life. Create a space for yourself to flesh out ideas and map out ways to turn them into action.

CALL TO ACTION

I challenge you to learn more about the way your state or country runs the education system. These are the people who have been voted in as district representatives in your state and ultimately write and pass the bills by which we all live. Speak with your lawmakers on how to execute new policies and standards in your community.

CHAPTER 10

SERIOUS INQUIRIES ONLY: THE DEBATE ON CAREER READINESS AND REPRESENTATION

———

"Intelligence without ambition is a bird without wings."
— SALVADOR DALÍ

"People learn who they are by the images of themselves, the representations that they seek."
— HARRY LENNIX

What are the requirements for building a community?

As I continue to wonder about why school runs the way it does, I realize our curriculum, our focus, and our objectives are missing two key things that help foster a sense of belonging: career readiness and representation.

School teaches us the "what" instead of the "why" and dictates the message content is king—not customization. Learning the same thing as the person next to you won't have any magical effect other than meeting grade level standards and preparing to be "college-ready."

We'll get into hacking college in a later chapter. First, I want you to deconstruct what career, readiness, and representation mean to you (not the dictionary definitions).

CAREER:

READINESS:

REPRESENTATION:

As you fill in those definitions, remember the uniqueness of your point of view: where you have grown up has shaped your view of the world and where you want to end up has created your image of the future. However, the problem is that none of our definitions, not even mine, truly encompasses what school is and what it should be. But, when we put all our definitions together, we can step back and see a clearer picture.

For us to have these meanings, we must have everyone's voices present and minds open to the variations of how we each see the world.

**

The National Association of Colleges and Employers defines career readiness as "the attainment and demonstration of requisite competencies that broadly prepare college graduates for a successful transition into the workplace. These competencies are critical thinking and problem solving by exercising sound reasoning to analyze issues, making decisions, and overcoming problems."[49]

Does any of that sound familiar to you?

Being "ready," or prepared for the future, involves an effective transition into a diverse environment that will push you to ask tough questions (like how to do something, or why it is being done) and dissect the purpose of an action with regard to whom it will affect.

Google University defines representation as "the action of speaking or acting on behalf of someone or the state of being so represented." I believe career readiness must align with the objectives of the classroom and the avenues of representation are what exemplify that class.

As a student raised to equally embrace and appreciate my two different cultures as a Nigerian-American, I know the importance of seeing people who look like you excel in their fields. The value of having a Black, Asian, Hispanic, or Native American teacher challenges the homogeneity of the current teacher field and material. Teachers are influential people in our lives and having someone from your community help

---

49   National Association of Colleges and Employers. "Career Readiness Defined."

you reach a goal or solve a problem can significantly change your worldview.

Their presence alone can serve as a constant reminder that you have a piece of comfort and support to help elevate you in times of need.

Because all these groups have unique life experiences, the impact of being represented and seeing others represented makes you understand the importance of diversity— new insights!

You can actualize your potential when you realize through others who have changed the narrative to show that anything is possible.

Think about yourself in reading this book. This is a type of representation. High school students rarely get to have a say when it comes to education leadership and thought books, yet here we are—experiencing what the future of high school looks like through the lens of a high schooler.

Hypothetical situations never did anyone any good either. We can't pretend to benefit from what we don't see. As the saying goes, you cannot give what you do not have. The same is true for representation; if we don't have teachers who look like us, what inspires students of color to consider teaching as a career?

School does not teach us to have role models outside of our textbooks, when the real action often happens outside of those blue walls. However, I have found the most unconventional teachers are the ones without a Bachelor's Degree in Education and a subject specialty.

How are we sure that these four years of schooling have a tangible impact on our futures in the current way we navigate through it?

∗∗

Over fifty years ago, former President John F. Kennedy said, "We choose to go to the moon not because it is easy, but because it is hard." These words reverberate the concept of a key learning technique called moonshot thinking. You probably have heard of other phrases like "shoot for the moon" or "reach for the stars." Moonshot thinking is a type of **thinking** which aims to achieve something generally believed to be impossible.[50]

Astro Teller, an acclaimed computer scientist, paints this scenario: "You would not and do not spend your time, or even half of your day, being bothered that you currently cannot teleport from here to Japan. That is because there is a part of you that thinks and believes it is impossible. *Moonshot thinking is choosing to be bothered by that.*"[51]

Richard DeVaul, a rapid prototyping specialist, sees it like this: "While everyone else is working on improving the 10% of an issue or challenge, you're problem-solving for ten times the change that is required for real progress." By taking

---

50 Capaldi, Edward. "What is Moonshot Thinking." YouTube, September 13, 2017.
51 Ibid.

seemingly huge risks, you help to bring about the inspiring changes that we have seen today, from the invention of the airplane to building prosthetics limbs.

Prototyping is a draft version of a product that allows you to explore your ideas and show the intention behind a feature or the overall design concept to users before investing time and money into development.[52]

Teller goes on to say, "When Kennedy said we would put a man on the moon, it's about the fact that he said, 'We don't know how to do this yet and we're gonna do it anyway.' That sent chills up everybody's spine because if that happens *what can't we do?*"[53]

You may recall being asked as a child what you wanted to be when you grew up. I personally have always been bothered by this question because after asking children that, those looking for a response would put up a list of options to choose from as if we did not have the creativity to make up or know careers ourselves.

A list might have appeared as helpful to some; however, it also limited the direction in which I thought the possibilities could go. What if I wanted to become an author, computer scientist, or dare I say, entrepreneur?

Everyone knows a kid or was the kid who said they wanted to be an astronaut when they grew up. However, without much

---

52   Usability.Gov. "Prototyping."

53   Capaldi, Edward. "What is Moonshot Thinking." YouTube, September 13, 2017.

thought, that idea was likely discarded and seen as frivolous and childish at best. Today, kids are saying they want to be a Twitch streamer, or YouTuber, which just shows how our ideas change with different generations.[54]

Moonshot thinking takes this framework of thought and asks us to come up with a problem we want to solve and ideally the right technology to pursue the solution. Moonshot thinking asks that same kid, why can't you be an astronaut? Why can't you be a YouTuber?

However, here's the real problem: asking kids to choose what they want to spend their adult lives doing with little knowledge and exposure to real options is irresponsible and ineffective.

Most kids will not choose to pursue the answer they provide their teacher. Even so, the phrase "ever since I was a kid, I knew I wanted to be x" can prevent people from going outside of what they believe is their intended career path.

Where I grew up, we had only seen a small breadth of cliché careers to pick from—doctor, lawyer, or engineer. I call these common careers "the three hoops." Now, don't be mistaken, these three hoops are great careers and people in those fields have done sufficient work to advance humanity. However, when examining the people who have actually shaken and rewired the system to produce innovative and effective products commonly used today, there

---

54   Kinseth, Amanda. "Digital Future: The Youtuber Age - What Kids Want To Be When They Grow Up." WPDE.

is a pattern of difference and thought beyond conventional perspectives.

The world would be a very boring place if there were only three areas where we might have an impact.

Moonshot thinking pushes us to think and develop new strategies for solving a known problem. We can use that volition to come up with a solution that is ten times more efficient than what anyone has ever imagined.

Adam Grant, professor of psychology at the University of Pennsylvania advises, "Don't ask kids what they want to be when they grow up. It encourages them to define themselves in terms of work. Instead, ask them what they want to do— and who they want to be. You can aspire to be a person of integrity and generosity in any career."[55]

Even so, the surveys and interviews that Stanford professor William Damon has conducted indicate that "only about one in five young people in the twelve-to-twenty-two-year age range express a clear vision of where they want to go, what they want to accomplish in life, and why. Almost sixty percent may have engaged in some potentially purposeful activities, or they may have developed some vague aspirations, but they do not have any real commitment to such activities or any realistic plans for pursuing their aspirations."[56]

55   Grant, Adam (@AdamMGrant). "Don't ask kids what." Twitter, April 3, 2019.
56   Haskell, Kristie. "Preparing Students For Life?" National Association of Independent Schools.

What is the purpose of a list if the choice does not have experience behind it? Discovering what we want to do when we "grow up" involves a process of finding a problem to solve and believing in our motivation to solve it.

As Miracle Olatunji says in her book, *Purpose: How to Live and Lead With Impact*, **passion = curiosity + experience + action**.[57]

However, once again—and I say this with irony—when we have taken the time to think of a problem to solve, sometimes we run into yet another problem: action.

The most difficult part of branching out is creating the blueprint for the launch. My stages of thought are as follows:

1. How can I get started? When should I get started? Actually, when is the latest possible time for me to get this thing started?
2. Who do I tell about my idea? What is the best way to include this concept into my current conversations? When should I stop asking questions?
3. Okay, okay, okay. I can do this. Wait, how much money will I make? Sorry, how much money does it take to make this project a reality? How long do I have to work on this?

---

57 Olatunji, Miracle. *Purpose: How To Live and Lead With Impact*. New Degree Press, 2019.

4. Alright, who should start this with me? Do I need anyone's help? Where can I find the help I need?
5. CAN I EVEN DO THIS? Who before me has done this and has been successful? What are the odds I will succeed? Slim to none or at least a 50/50 shot?
6. S.O.S.: Whom can I personally look to for help and inspiration?!

The last question is where the thought process gets interesting. After fretting about the entire plan and wondering if it is even worth designing, I find myself always asking this: is there anyone who looks like me or who was in a similar situation that I can be motivated by? In my experience, this was a great way to build community and learn about new opportunities.

**

The representation of a woman with dark, brown skin and 4C curly hair with a Nigerian background is an image I rarely came across as a young girl. The people who did exceptional things were the same color as the men in my American history books: you guessed it, White.

In the small chance the next chapter in the book would be highlighting a pioneer of color, I spent most of my childhood hoping I could go through one of those hoops and become a hero for another Black child in the United States. I thought if I didn't become a doctor, a different path wouldn't have the same kind of significance in American history. But none of the females who inspired me—Lupita Nyong'o, Chimamanda Ngozi Adichie, Gloria Bamiloye, Oprah Winfrey, and Gabby

Douglas—took a "common hoop" route of unleashing their potential; they still managed to inspire me!

Imagine what that does for someone who never feels like they could ever be "career-ready" to see stories of success without having to follow a rigid set of rules and expectations. A study from *SAGE Journals* on Educational Evaluation and Policy Analysis found a correlation between same-race teachers and reduced rates of exclusionary discipline and willful defiance among Black students at all grade levels.[58] Students will listen and respond when they see teachers listening and responding in a way that understands them.

Another study from the University of Chicago Press Journals found that schools with more black teachers and leadership also had more black students in gifted programs.[59]

Some people think representation is not as big a deal to the learning environment as a whole or to college/career readiness specifically. However, having a diverse platform for students to cultivate their own interests and projects to pursue stems from initiating open and inclusive conversations.

Danai Gurira, the actress who portrayed General Okoye in *Black Panther*, elaborated on this with an example of the kind of thought a young Black girl can have with this

---

58   Lindsay, Constance A. and Cassandra M. D. Hart. "Exposure To Same-Race Teachers And Student Disciplinary Outcomes For Black Students In North Carolina." *SAGE Journals* 39, no. 3 (2017): 485-510.

59   Grissom, Jason A., Luis A. Rodriguez, and Emily C. Kern. "Teacher And Principal Diversity And The Representation Of Students Of Color In Gifted Programs: Evidence From National Data." *The Elementary School Journal* 117, no. 3 (2017): 396-422.

representation. She says, "If little girls have that and have images now to refer to that are cool and empowered and hip, that they can say, 'Listen, I don't have to fall into anyone else's ideology of what I can be,' and that's everything. That's just everything."[60]

There is no doubt that after time, speaking with the same person or group of people about how to generate engaging content will be met with dull feedback which changes slightly after each session. Like writing a paper, as time progresses, you will not be able to catch the errors in your own work because you've become comfortable with the idea being the best it can be, even though there is a high chance it is not.

Therefore, you need to get many people to offer their opinions and critiques. You'll want representative feedback in order to create a better and more substantial product. Representation of more than one voice allows all contributors to benefit.

In addition, concepts and products tailored to basic and general audiences are not representative of the learners in the classroom. Plus, they often don't benefit anyone.

In fact, Senator Lockman notes, "There are studies that show that all children benefit from having a diverse array of educators as long as those educators care about and connect with them. Without a doubt, there is a negative effect on students to never see a person of color at the front of the room. And that's on all students, especially the white students." Despite

---

60 Lawson, Kimberly. "Why Seeing Yourself Represented On Screen Is So Important." *VICE*, February 20, 2018.

popular belief, it is evident diversity is the catalyst between a moonshot and the actual target. In order to gain momentum and put together a system or solution that helps humanity, you must consult **all** humanity—not just White men in designer suits.

People of different cultures, races, and backgrounds have voices too. Choosing not to include and provide avenues for diversity of thought hurts the entire classroom dynamic and contradicts the definition of career-readiness.

I cannot dismiss the contributions some of my favorite teachers have made to inspire me to disrupt the narrative that my skin color symbolizes barriers and limits. However, there is absolutely nothing more empowering than having someone with whom you can aspire to model and connect with.

In imitating greatness, all of us can find our own elements of distinction and authenticity.

The power of representation is similar to the concept of moonshot thinking in that both concepts rely on adding more to the existing ideas.

Essentially, when you put yourself out there, you've begun the intricate process of designing your own framework—one you may be incredibly unsure of, but are extremely motivated by. In order to prepare yourself for the real world, you must:

- Be excited about being uncomfortable, whether it has to do with talking to someone who is different from you or trying out a new technique no one has ever proposed or thought of before

- Demand more representation of other students' identities so you can be prepared to interact with the infinite possibilities of collaboration
- Find areas in your life that need to moonshot and CATAPULT!

The final note on career readiness: Stephen Guise, an internationally bestselling author, sums up the idea perfectly, "You can get straight A's in school, but nobody, no matter how successful, gets straight A's in life. No, in life, you tend to get A's by getting F's first. Lots and lots of F's." The only way to get F's is to move away from baby steps and move forward into giant slings that will teach you lessons you'll value for life.

TAKEAWAYS & LESSONS:

- By adding diverse voices and expanding the mind on the possibilities that can be reached, new and worthwhile investments in human capital can be accomplished.
- It is with inclusive thought that education can become revolutionary in all our lives.
- The most important moonshots are the ones that boldly fail over and over and over again, relentlessly ready to learn and fail again the next day.
- Being career-ready means embracing difference, uncertainty, and the unbelievable growth that comes along with it. And sometimes, implementing this embrace is better late than never.

CALL TO ACTION

I challenge you to attend an interest group meeting, club, organization, or program with people who do not look like you. For example, a book reading from an author in the area or a school club that seeks to raise awareness on underrepresented groups. Show up for your fellow lovely humans!

CHAPTER 11

"LATE" IS BETTER THAN NEVER

"It's not the days in your life, but the life in your days that counts."

— BRIAN WHITE

"It's never too late - never too late to start over, never too late to be happy."

— JANE FONDA

We have all gone through times in our lives where the timing of our actions was not as "on point" as it could have been.

Being late is a feeling that can crush you, whether that is turning a project in hours past the deadline, asking for help, or recognizing your own flaws. Out of this conquerable weight comes the realization that knowing where you stood at that late moment was better than wallowing in blissful ignorance.

If you hadn't turned in the project at all, it would have resulted in a zero.

If you hadn't asked for help, your grade or understanding of the topic would have continued to plummet as the material got more complex.

Without recognizing our own flaws, we cannot take knowledgeable steps toward addressing them and making our strengths stronger.

I want to show you there is no deadline for success or agency in your learning—if you do not set limited parameters for yourself.

You must recognize that growth as a student, peer, person, friend, and contributor to society takes time. No one emerges from the womb with academic, social, or athletic prowess.

Instead, it is best to have the awareness of your own development, so when it's time to make tough decisions—such as what path to pursue, what mentor to choose, what class to drop, and what professional to shadow—you will make those decisions as they specifically pertain to you.

Lateness has often been attributed to teenagers as the demise of our entire age group; however, this chapter spans beyond your high school experience. The lack of urgency you might feel toward a subject, activity, or event can be a great indicator of your level of attention and apathy. If you don't care about it, you likely will not take the conscious steps to change your habits of lateness.

However, when you identify the areas of your life currently suffering from this lack of urgency, you can start a path toward emergence, acceptance, and fulfillment.

I started to come to terms with my time management during my freshman year. The time where everything feels like a fresh and new beginning; however, you don't realize the significance of the year until it's over. I noticed in certain classes, like math and civics, that my attention toward learning had peaked in the first semester. My GPA was coasting along the line of what my college counselor would consider concerning and I couldn't highlight the gaps in my learning.

I was frustrated because I felt like I was underachieving and that my freshman year had become a giant step back, instead of a small, but significant step toward my undiscovered future. I had a GPA problem (I thought after getting my midterm exam results) and moving past the fact that freshman year was an easy blast for my peers, I asked some upperclassmen for advice.

I worked to understand the problem, accepted that the numbers were permanent but not staining, and worked at grasping concepts to learn them rather than fretting over a three-digit number.

A junior—we'll call him Arjan for privacy purposes—told me then about how his freshman year ultimately shook him and gave him a real-life wake-up call. He finished second semester with final grades that equated to a 2.8 GPA. He told me he didn't care about anything except for hanging out with his friends, going to parties, and having "fun" in class. This isn't to say that any of those activities are bad, but he admitted that the excessive quantity to which he did these things replaced his attention toward learning.

Fortunately for Arjan, he chose to turn things around sophomore year by seeking help as needed, turning in assignments, and communicating with his peers about subjects that went beyond "What are you doing this afternoon?" I learned a lot from what he had gone through and realized my own situation was just a matter of seeing where I needed help and looking at it from a different perspective.

He used his own story to motivate others that it is never too late to choose a different direction.

However, it will be detrimental if you blindly ignore the fact you need to emerge from the lateness, accept the outcome of your actions, and fulfill your greatest potential from this awareness.

"Time agency" is how the process of independence and retraining your mind begins. Once you understand that getting started involves emergence, acceptance, and fulfillment, you can find what Wisconsin high school student Morgan Klug calls "shock value." Shock value happens with intentionality and individuality.

Time agency is taking control of your day, week, year, and life. It means seeing your high school experience day by day and planning out the steps to execute your goals in the most effective way. Shock value is what sets you apart from others and often makes you feel surer of who you are.

Try pinpointing your shock value by answering these sentences out loud:

- What does it mean to be (insert your name)?
- What makes you, you?
- What wouldn't you be you without? What absence of qualities or desires would take away from your shock value?
- What are you CRAZY about?

To be me, Deborah, means constantly reevaluating how to help, how to make a situation better, and how to troubleshoot an unexpected outcome. I am Deborah because I enjoy talking about what's going on in the world from healthcare to politics to trending technology. I wouldn't be myself without my burning desire to find the answer to the question, "Who decides?" because in a world where we have all the resources, we—the students, the leaders of tomorrow, today, and now—need to be the ones making decisions. I am CRAZY about student agency and allowing people to recognize the fullest extent of their impact. That's my shock value.

Morgan told me about her defining qualities and the activities that make Morgan, Morgan. She's a part of the Wisconsin Youth Apprentice Program, a state government-led initiative which enables students to use their time to experience hands-on jobs in technical fields. According to the Society for Human Resource Management, less than five percent of U.S. secondary-school students take part in apprenticeships.[61]

This is a shame, especially since the program gives students real career experience by putting them directly in the field. What's more, they get paid, receive course credit, and get to miss class! Morgan is a bank teller, so she has been able to learn about 401k plans, mortgages, and auto loans. She has also learned that while she now knows about how to do her own taxes, she doesn't want to handle people's money. To Morgan, this was important because she believes "it's a really interesting way to give students an upper hand. If they're interested in something, then give them an opportunity to partner with a corporation, a company, or even a small business, to work on something they are potentially interested in going into in the future."

Her key takeaways from her apprenticeship had to do with acting now so "late" does not even have to happen.

"I don't want to be the loan officer, I don't want to be the bank teller, and I don't want to be the mortgage person," Morgan declares.

If you can figure out a field you're interested in and then later find out you wouldn't want to spend your life on that career path, you'll save years of your life just from that experience.

---

61   Tomaka, Lauren. "States In Region Investing More In Apprenticeship Programs." The Council of State Governments.

You can eliminate entire areas of impact that don't fascinate you after seeing what it would be like to have that job.

Even if you're a junior or senior in high school, it is never too late to find your interests through an apprenticeship, internship, or other hands-on, long-duration, exploration program.

"This is something that students are losing, the ability to have professional relationships and have both conversation and communication skills. The ability to talk to other people or talk in front of other people is so vital. These kinds of skills equip you to be a better candidate in professional fields."

– MORGAN KLUG

Act and turn "late" into genius with the PB & G strategy:

- partner with companies and corporations
- build professional relationships with adults
- gain financial information

These three skills can help you to retrain the way you view your personal path to success. The earlier you learn these ideas the better.

**

On the topic of finances, Brazilian educator Paulo Freire talks about acquiring information like a banking system. He elaborates on a concept of education in which "knowledge is a gift bestowed by those who consider themselves knowledgeable upon those whom they consider to know nothing." In this view, Freire claims that by assuming the roles of teachers as depositors and students as receptors, the banking concept thereby changes humans into objects.[62]

When you put coins into a piggy bank, you have the assumption that it needs to continue receiving money until it's full. You never have the expectation that the piggy will ever spit the coins out by itself or make a complaint about how many or how few coins are inserted on a weekly basis.

When we continue to take in the tips and the pointers of how to become more valuable "cointributors" to society, the piggy in this scenario represents us!

Don't get me wrong, a piggy bank coming to life would be frightening, but this addresses the problem of the passiveness in education and urges action for students in the application of their futures. You could be extremely interested a job, but you've never really immersed yourself in that field.

Why haven't you?

---

62 Micheletti, Gabrielle. "Re-Envisioning Paulo Freire's 'Banking Concept Of Education.'" *Inquiries Journal* 2, no. 2 (2010): 1.

We can no longer be piggy banks, waiting for someone else to cash in on our knowledge. We get into more experiential forms of learning that enable us to engage with the world and learn about ourselves.

TAKEAWAYS & LESSONS:

- Coming to terms with your flaws and gaps in understanding yields solutions, not more problems.
- Find your shock value and exercise it in every area of your life both outside and inside of school!
- Turn "late" into the PB & G power method mentioned above: partner, build, and gain.
- Invest in your resilience or toughness to recover from momentary sadness of failure. You can work toward finding ways to succeed, which will aid you in building character, rather than solely focusing on the content.

CALL TO ACTION

I challenge you to take on at least one week of field experience (during the school year or the summer) in a career field that excites you. What was the first one you thought of when you read that last sentence? Choose that one!

- I spent two weeks looking at bioengineering and realized how essential it is in the healthcare system and my future patients' lives. I am pursing nursing, but want to pursue research into prosthetics through a partnership with a bioengineer. You might find a spark in exploring a new path or note a career choice you don't want to pursue anymore.

- Either way, by taking on the experience, you will expand your network, retrain your mind about the field, and immerse yourself in what it would look like to work in the chosen profession (and you are allowed to not be in love with it)!

CHAPTER 12

CHARACTER-BUILDING: THE POWER OF GRIT

———

"The function of education is to teach one to think intensively and to think critically. Intelligence plus character - that is the goal of true education."

— DR. MARTIN LUTHER KING, JR.

"Personality can open doors, but only character can keep them open."

— ELMER G. LETTERMAN

I believe the best method to developing your character involves reevaluating what your impact is and what it means for you to have a voice.

After all, we experience content daily from our phone screens to our never-ending to-do lists. How we react to these sources of information has molded us into the people we are today.

There is a disparity between the information we are consuming and the action we are taking.

In our classrooms, teachers have the perfect opportunity to be a catalyst for many of us who cannot see past the end of the school day. But when they have to consider how to use nine months of seven-hour days, the fact of the matter is there's just not enough time: not enough time to fully connect with their hundred plus students, not enough time to accomplish all of the material, and certainly not enough time to teach *character*.

We spend most of our adolescent and teenage years in class, but there are many places outside of the classroom where we learn character—from sports teams to academic clubs and projects. The habitual action of coming and going from class has become ingrained in who we are, which is why it can be hard to find ourselves and our shock value.

I want you to look at the world from those two viewpoints: consumption of content and consciousness of character.

We learn and take in both essential and nonessential knowledge at a rapid pace daily. Sorting through all the information has become second nature to me; I see my thoughts from a scale of urgency.

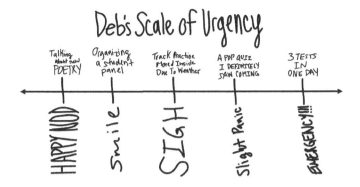

Deb's Scale of Urgency

Talking about new POETRY | Organizing a student panel | Track Practice Moved Inside Due To Weather | A POP QUIZ I DEFINITELY SAW COMING | 3 TESTS IN ONE DAY

HAPPY NOD | Smile | SIGH | Slight Panic | EMERGENCY!!!

However, when it comes to developing your immediate reaction to how the world works with the essential information, this process can be much slower. Character is both an art form and a mirror of our mental and moral capabilities.

By creating a balance of both aspects, your high school experience will transform from a mere four-year journey into the start of life-long reflection.

**

Today, we face the unending peril of perfection as we venture through our own trials and difficulties in the education system. By fielding us with questions about the future, educators can start to realize life presents many challenging issues which vary from child to child; the methods we individually use to solve those problems can help in the long run.

Rather than teaching us the check-box method of acquiring what we desire, active problem-solving can instead show us how to persevere and think differently to achieve our goals, even if it means creating those problems ourselves.

We need to stop checking boxes and start creating or adding to categories of our own. The idea of this determination stems from a concept called grit. Character and grit are like two long-lost friends. You can have one for a while, but eventually, they will find a way to reconnect.

*"The **character** of a person or place consists of all the qualities they have that make them distinct from others."*[63]

Grit as Angela Duckworth—psychologist, author, and professor at the University of Pennsylvania—defines character as a "passion and perseverance for very long-term goals, having the stamina, and sticking with your future, day in, day out, not just for the week, not just for the month, but for years, and working really hard to make that future a reality."[64] The key thing with grit is understanding the long-term goal and the steps required to fully pursue it.

However, the missing piece of grit is the empowerment of students to push back against the status quo and breaking the "glass ceiling" everyone talks about.

The truth is this metaphorical glass ceiling cannot be seen or broken without understanding why it should be targeted in the first place. You must identify the barrier in order to disrupt it. By examining the obstacles that will inevitably or surprisingly occur in the problem-solving procedure, we

---

63 Collins Dictionary. "Character Definition And Meaning."
64 Duckworth, Angela. "Grit: The power of passion and perseverance." TED video, 6:07. Posted April 2013.

can then choose between our grit to persevere through the challenge or waiting for someone else to fix the mess.

You're not always going to be a Glad Garrett about certain situations; sometimes you'll be a Debby Downer, whether it happens consciously or without recognition. These two different groups can be characterized as the "gritters" and the "grovelers." I see these terms in the sense that grovelers are usually bogged down by content while gritters push through the content with the goal of building character. Grit is to persevere; grovel is to crawl.

Those with grit see the areas of difficulty and tackle them head-on, while those who grovel, or complain, choose to neglect the issue until it requires immediate attention. Even then, they enlist someone else to do the job for them. Like I said in the previous chapter on lateness, you have to come to terms with the goals you seek to accomplish, so you can contribute to your purpose in a meaningful way.

Those with grit follow the near identical steps of a skilled entrepreneur by generating interest in the thing they cannot seem to care for and by researching and gaining more knowledge on the topic.

Then, they generate a *deep* interest in the thing they cannot seem to care for. This is not an easy step, which is why it is visited twice.

The gritters must discover and deepen their interest in the chosen topic before moving forward. The grovelers tend to aim toward passing through subjects "just to get it done."

Duckworth continues the point that once we have fostered an interest, then we can do the kind of difficult and sometimes frustrating practice that makes us even better: "Maintaining a sense of hope or resilience, even when there are setbacks."[65] It is crucial to stay open to reflection, criticism, and vulnerability during the numerous setbacks that will happen. Owning your struggles equates to a sort of mental cognition or toughness, helping you realistically redesign your technique to achieve your goals, like Arjan! Duckworth calls this trait being "extraordinarily meta-cognitive."

Now, I can go into meta-cognition and discuss its role in the education system, but I cannot gloss over the other part of this analogy—groveling. To grovel by the dictionary definition means "to beg incessantly." When you are a groveler, you don't want to make efforts for yourself, rather you use your power to persuade someone else to complete or solve problems for you.

The act of groveling isn't heavily associated with the education system; some see this method of reception as a necessary factor for gaining a skill, securing a grade, or achieving an award.

I looked up grovel and found an image of a small cartoon person with a large, pink tongue, salivating all over the brown dress shoe of a corporate leader. If you have ever received a failing mark in a class or forgot to pull your weight on a group project, this image depicts what it looks like when you ask for a second chance or forgiveness.

---

65   Ibid.

Everyone has done this at a point in their lives and there is no shame in being a past groveler.

So, how do I know if I am a gritter or a groveler and how can I use this information to help develop my character?

Inspired from Angela Duckworth's grit quiz, I decided to create my own quiz on the idea of grit or grovel; I promise this is the only exam in this book. Circle the numbers for the statements you identify with, then score it.

**

Scoring: You will assess your two scores separately. Questions 1, 3, 5, 7, and 9 relate to grovel score. Questions 2, 4, 6, 8, and 10 relate to your grit score.

For questions 1-10, assign the following points:

1 = *Not like me at all*
2 = *Not much like me*
3 = *Somewhat like me*
4 = *Mostly like me*
5 = *Very much like me*

THE GRIT OR GROVEL QUIZ

	Not at all	Not much	Some what	Mostly	Very much
1. I enjoy a good challenge... sometimes.	1	2	3	4	5
2. I ask for help when I need it.	1	2	3	4	5
3. I rely on others to complete the ideas I create.	1	2	3	4	5
4. Creating is a key passion of mine.	1	2	3	4	5
5. I spend most of my time on schoolwork and don't have time for problem-solving.	1	2	3	4	5
6. New experiences always find me. From them, I seek more.	1	2	3	4	5
7. I set too many goals and often get frustrated.	1	2	3	4	5
8. I embrace failure and the prospect of having to start over.	1	2	3	4	5
9. My interests are mainly based on what is taught to me in class.	1	2	3	4	5
10. My attention can be focused on a variety of topics.	1	2	3	4	5

Add up all your grovel points (maximum is 25 points) and divide by five. Add up all your grit points (maximum is 25 points) and divide by seven. The higher score of the two is your current status as a gritter or groveler.

UYIG SCORE CARD			
Grovel Score		**Grit Score**	
1	—	2	—
3	—	4	—
5	—	6	—
7	—	8	—
9	—	10	—
Total Score: / 5		Total Score: / 7	
Higher Score (in decimals):			

Share your results with your family and friends!

**

Those with bursting barrels of grit can share their stories with people who have not yet grasped the value of this concept.

Zach Jones of Dual School compellingly related these ideas in his thought, "I envision a world in which people feel **collective ownership to educate the people** nearby them, which would make companies and organizations become accustomed to helping students and own their collective ownership to help the students by enabling their ideas. We need communities getting behind schools."

When we collectively acknowledge as a group that we must take steps toward improvement, we actively exercise agency and enact purposeful change.

When I realized my personal brand of being an igniter and wanting to help others become powerful in their education, I took collective ownership of my community and the education world.

When you decide the best way to show your character is in growing to help others grow, you will find more fulfillment in your environment, your own personal brand, and your ability to impact.

**

Every single student in the education system, regardless of what school they attend, is brimming with gritty potential.

If schools are really at the forefront of building hubs for students to have grit, then there must be more experiments on the possibilities of impact. If we want to demonstrate that schools can be centers for building character and cultivating grit-minded geniuses, it starts with focus. The focus needs to go beyond the content and more toward the lessons students will take with them to collectively own the innovation in education.

We can either complain about a situation or we can work together with our community to disrupt the current course of the stagnant, one-sided education system. With good character and fearless grit, we must also embrace the roles of respecting and advocating for the ever-changing education process.

TAKEAWAYS & LESSONS:

- Character-building takes empathy. Find interest in what you learn and then take it a step further by having a conversation and initiating research or a project centered on sparking that interest in others.
- We must have collective ownership over innovation in education and create avenues to bring more people to the decision table.
- Grit starts with identifying a problem and persevering through to find a solution. Gritters choose to work on ideas that affect their communities and spur change.
- Recognize you don't have to "start all over." If you have been content-minded before, use that knowledge. You can always take your current experience and make it better by adding an intentional layer of exploration, curiosity, and connection. That's the beginning of integration!

CALL TO ACTION

I challenge you to share your results from the grit or grovel quiz with me on Instagram or Twitter (@deb_olatunji) with the #gritorgrovelquiz tag. Take a picture of yourself with the book and tell me:

- What your thoughts are about your results?
- What steps of progress you will take in the future and who you are going to bring along with you?

CHAPTER 13

THE CONSEQUENCES OF "WE": INTEGRATION THAT EXCITES

———

"One day our descendants will think it incredible that we paid so much attention to things like the amount of melanin in our skin or the shape of our eyes or our gender instead of the unique identities of each of us as complex human beings."

— FRANKLIN THOMAS

"It is not more bigness that should be our goal. We must attempt, rather, to bring people back to the warmth of community, to the worth of individual effort and responsibility and of individuals working together as a community, to better their lives and their children's future."

— ROBERT F. KENNEDY

How familiar are you with the word community? What about integration?

To all my future engineers out there, you're incredibly amazing already, but you can put your hands down because I am not talking about circuits.

I define integration to mean taking incremental or large steps toward unifying a particularly excluded community or group. The differences of the excluded group are usually related to their diversity of thought, beliefs, skin color, sexuality, and age. "Integration that excites" pushes for the awareness that our differences should connect and fascinate us, rather than divide us.

This process involves passing around the torch of input in discussions about topics like reforming education. You still have your own embers to help ignite the spark, but not enough embers to light the fire.

After reading this book, I want you to become a fearless firestarter (metaphorically, of course) with other people who are willing and excited to create change and dialogue on issues that matter.

I also want to show you that joining in with people doesn't mean forsaking your beliefs, value, or purpose. Community builds you up in a way isolation never will because it takes away the "me factor" and replaces it with the "we factor."

"Me factor" only advocates for personal motives, progress, and growth. "We factor" puts the wonder in wonderful

*by including interpersonal relationships. Through the integrations of race, innovation, thought, and growth, we can build a world that relies on community to thrive and **redesign**. These qualities will reflect in both conquering the classroom and retraining your mind—moving you closer to embrace utilizing the outside world.*

Integration has held many meanings in the past decades or two. In terms of race, tapping into diverse groups of people is one way to start. Or, you can make a point to include the voices of varying races when making decisions affecting the entire population. And if you don't know, ask!

Talking about race in school causes people to be uncomfortable; however, in order to cultivate communities of collaboration, these conversations need to happen.

**

In the fall of my senior year, my high school administration decided to invite an organization that focuses on solving conflicts through interactive consulting to have a DEI (diversity, equity, and inclusion) conversation with different grade levels. I sat close to the presenters, shifting around in my red-velvet seat as I watched my classmates respond to stories of racial conflict in schools. In some cases, it was hard to believe the experiences the students had gone through.

On the presentation, an Asian student held a sign with a microaggression about stereotypically smelling like rice. People around me chorused the words "I had never heard of that one before."

Microaggressions are often racially charged "subtle blows," but over time they can take a toll on mental and physical health.[66]

As more students' posters showed ignorant and racist comments, members of the audience couldn't help but double over in laughter.

My first thought was that their reaction came from a place of disbelief, but after a while it didn't seem this was the case. In the past, I have heard stinging comments about my race like *you know, you're pretty for a black girl* or *wow! you speak so well!* as if my skin color equated to the lack of beauty or the inability to fully comprehend and communicate. Seeing the reactions of the surrounding laughter made me feel like the presentation opened a window to the topic of race, but didn't open the door and invite us in to talk.

Through random selection, a few homerooms gathered in small groups to have a conversation. Out of the 972 students who attend my school, only twenty-eight percent of us had the opportunity to sit down and talk about race. I was not one of them.

When I think about solving racial injustice and breaking down the social boundaries keeping us from sharing our stories, I see a vivid presentation and a step further in the creation of small group discussions for everyone—not just a select number of students. By only hearing the outcry for

---

66 Dastagir, Alia E. "Microaggressions don't just 'hurt your feelings'." *USA Today,* February 28, 2018.

change and not examining the call for action, it takes away from the vulnerable experience of listening to a classmate's story or sharing your own. You should empathize with someone…not just sit uncomfortably for an hour and five minutes at seven in the morning.

These vital conversations refer to the practice of talking through how to break down our natural tendency to assume negative intentions about different ethnic groups based on our past knowledge or societal image of how other communities act. Passive generalization is not the same as investigative communication.

This fear of the "other" in our school communities causes tension in communication. It can also prevent us from asking the important question of "How can we?" instead of "Why should we?"

For example, in my experience, I haven't read many Native American stories, poems, plays, or novels in school. The question becomes:

How can we include the voices of Native American writers, poets, novelists, and playwrights in our English classes?

NOT

Why should we include the voices of Native American writers, poets, novelists, and playwrights in our English classes?

This applies to all your classes and personal activities that fill your day. Your individual growth from a supportive community comes from the diversity you immerse yourself in and the hard conversations you are willing (or scared) to have. It's good if you feel uncomfortable because then we can do something to address that feeling.

I could write an entire memoir on the importance of classroom culture when it comes to race, innovation, thought, and growth, but the real idea here is that we must share these great launchpads for success.

**

Jono Bacon, author of *The Art of Community: Building the New Age of Participation*, has a personal blog about a concept called the collaboration-driven ethos.

This is not the same ethos, logos, and pathos you may have learned or are yet to learn about in school.

Bacon clarifies this phrase, collaboration-driven ethos, as "an excitement about what is possible when you get a group of people together who share a common ethos and a commitment to furthering it."[67]

You have a goal, but you know that it can be more successful when you collaborate with like-minded individuals to make it happen.

---

67 Bacon, Jono. "The Art Of Community, Second Edition." O'Reilly | Safari Books Online.

He encourages you to think of it like this: "Community is fundamentally a soft science. Compare it with, for example, programming. If you want to write a computer software application, you write it in a programming language. These synthetic languages are vessels of logic. They live and breathe in a world where the answer to a question is either yes or no; there is no maybe."[68]

We work together as a unit, balancing between consensus and disagreement. Either we're championing a diversity community, or we're not; there is no in-between. That's why building a sense of belonging is so crucial to experiencing high school to its fullest and retraining your mind to acknowledge the value of your community.

This connection of social capital affects your ability to navigate between "me" and "we."

Author Lyda Hanifan referred to social capital as "those tangible assets [that] count for most in the daily lives of people: namely goodwill, fellowship, sympathy, and social intercourse among the individuals and families who make up a social unit."[69]

Your generation of positive social capital creates a standstill among your needs, but also gives people a real picture of how you interact with diversity and collective thinking.

---

68   Ibid.
69   OECD Insights: Human Capital. "What is social capital?" Organisation for Economic Co-operation and Development.

This ties into our duty to have the collective ownership over advancing education for all students, whether that is enhancing special education programs or having uncomfortable small-group conversations on race and ethnicity. It can also mean increasing efforts to make literacy better in your state and looking into how you can use your presence to create a beneficial classroom culture.

Inc. 500 entrepreneur and best-selling author Kevin Daum has seven steps you can take to start building a powerful community.[70] I will phrase them as questions you can answer to envision what they look like in action.

1. *"We" before "me"*: This seemingly elementary idea we have to put others before ourselves is a piece of advice which can help direct the peace when it comes to making decisions as a friend group, classroom, and community. **What's more important, voice or voices?**

2. *"Change the way things are"*: This is the conversation I keep having with legislators about education. If an approach isn't working, it needs to change! When the system is not getting better, it most likely is becoming worse, which means we need to act quickly to troubleshoot the issue and come up with a new solution. It helps to look at the issue from a different angle—think like an entrepreneur and experiment like a skateboarder! Invest in learning new skills that will help pave the path to a more efficient

---

70 Daum, Kevin. "7 Things You Have To Do To Build A Powerful Community." *Inc.*, February 17, 2017.

outcome. **What approaches aren't working and what is a new or redesigned concept that we can try?**

3. *"Fail fast; fail forward"*: The analysis of the grit vs. grovel argument can be applied to this statement. Don't fear failure, rather run into it over and over again to learn why the method isn't working. Redefine what it means to be a successful student in the twenty-first century and be okay with the definition. **How can we improve if we're not looking at where we went wrong and implementing how to TRY to accomplish AND learn more the next time around?**

4. *"Embrace discomfort. The impossible is possible"*: Be comfortable with UNCOMFORTABLE. If there were only one piece of advice I would want for you to take from this list, it would be being uncomfortable means you are taking a step in the right direction; stop keeping score and start keeping track of the number of risks you are fearfully taking toward making your community better. **Who's back needs to be scratched? How can you fearlessly reach toward and for what feels impossible?**

5. *"To thine own self be true"*: You don't have to be the best student, entrepreneur, astronaut, or [insert career path] to bring your community together and create change. Play to your strengths but also acknowledge the places in your life where you have weaknesses. Work toward what you can improve instead of trying to outdo yourself. **How can you use your own strengths to fuel the community fire?**

6. *"Luck is when preparation meets opportunity"*: Working together with others is what drives social capital, social impact, and social good. Prepare by having insightful conversations with people outside of your expertise. This way, you can learn more about different views of the issue to work together and solve it. **As U.S. Representative John Lewis said, "If not us, then who? If not now, then when?"**

7. *"Embrace a larger purpose"*: See where your community is struggling and respond by sharing your thoughts and welcome the ideas of others. Gary Vaynerchuk, Belarusian-American entrepreneur and internet personality, explains the weight of this last one best. "In a world where the odds of existing at all is practically zero, you are more likely to win the lottery TEN TIMES in your life than actually have one!"[71] You have been given the incredible opportunity to have an education and find a purpose. **In a world where you CAN DO what your heart desires, why not go after advancing and creating diverse communities near you?**

According to Eric Schaps from *Educational Leadership* magazine, "community building should become—at a minimum—a strong complement to the prevailing focus on academic achievement."[72] When you can prioritize having a community, and a good one in your life, you will find high school much more rewarding. You wouldn't want to play a sport or arrange music composition for a band all by yourself;

---

71 Onnit. "400 Trillion To One | Gary Vaynerchuk." YouTube, May 30, 2017.
72 Schaps, Eric. "Creating A School Community." *Educational* Leadership 60, no. 6 (2003): 31-33.

you know each person plays an important role in making projects go from idea to completion. Plus, it wouldn't be fun to kick a ball around or volley to yourself when you could have more fun with a friend or friends.

The consequences of integrating difference and uncomfortable conversations into your daily routine can help better shape your worldview, impact, and purpose.

Just as Robert Kennedy said "individuals working together as a community, to better their lives and their children's future" initiate change that can elevate generations to better resources and a greater quality and appreciation for life. Integration doesn't solely change your high school experience. Rather, it has the power to change your entire community and centers of positive influence...*influence that excites.*

TAKEAWAYS & LESSONS:
- In order to work through conflicts and differences, we need to start having meaningful discussions in small groups with our communities on the topic of race. These conversations can help resolve tensions, create solutions that consider all members of the community, and inform others on issues that they may never experience in their lives.
- Find ways to daily immerse yourself in diversity in a positive way.
- Go out and change the way things are. If you don't like something, you either change it or your mindset toward it.
- Be empowered to live a life with innovation, integration, and influence that excites. That's how you hack your mind

and the paths you'll take towards expanding it through college or your intended career.

CALL TO ACTION
I challenge you to build your social capital by utilizing the collaboration-driven ethos. Have an "excitement about what is possible when you get a group of people together who share a common goal and a commitment to *furthering it*."

CHAPTER 14

HACK COLLEGE ADMISSIONS: ENOUGH SAID.

———

"Stop waiting for permission to go get what you want."

— MEL ROBBINS

"It is no exaggeration to say that the current regime in elite college admissions has been far more successful in democratizing anxiety than opportunity."

— JEROME KARABEL

Senior year is the one year in high school that most students, teachers, and parents, believe matters most. However, if you look at the break-down of what usually happens in those four years, you will see that senior year is just the bowtie, rather than the present. College before you get in feels like crushing anxiety, but don't worry—I have a handful of friends I interviewed who testify otherwise.

The way I see it, in terms of the admissions process, you can alter your trajectory of high school up until the fall of your senior year. By then, most of your interests have been solidified, your next semester grades will be considered, and before you know it, you'll be heading off to college or directly into the workforce. You may have more interests that come as the year goes on, but in terms of your college application activities, longevity and consistency is something colleges and universities value over anything else.

I want to completely re-frame the importance of the college application journey. (And if you aren't planning on going to college immediately after high school, this change will still apply to you if or when you attend.)

In order to hack the college admissions process, you must know what it is, when to take certain testing steps, and ultimately how to stay true to your impact, support systems, and rate of return.

Freshmen Year:
- Exploration
- Year of self-interest (what do you like, what don't you like, what sparks you?)

Sophomore Year:
- Testing prep in advance: SAT and ACT or international examination process

- Utilize your mentors, teachers, peers, counselors, and parents
- Year of self-discovery (who are you, how can you propel your interests, how do your interests connect to who you are, how can your ideas guide you?)

Junior Year:
- Start college research in the fall
- Start thinking about a major: 80% of college students change their majors.[73] With that knowledge, find colleges that are flexible to change
- Year of self-realization (what knowledge have you learned that can help others, where can you grow, what's your personal brand, who are your connections, what do you enjoy spending your time on?)

Senior Year:
- If you plan on going to college, apply, and then throw a little party for yourself once you're done; if not, set up your post-graduation plans and then celebrate yourself too!
- Plan your time wisely and strategically have fun!
- Year of self-acceptance, self-love, and self-confidence

This is a basic idea of what those four years look like for most of us. Notice I didn't number any of it; these steps could fall in between any time period, from before the school year's beginning to the following summer.

---

73 Ramos, Yuritzy. "College Students Tend To Change Majors When They Find The One They Really Love." *Borderzine*, March 15, 2013.

The important part is the work gets done.

Unfortunately for the current twenty-first century admissions process, your test scores do matter to some extent depending on where you decide to attend. However, they do not define you. I repeat, **they DO NOT define you.**

I believe applying to college was never meant to be as much of a monopoly as it is today. Perhaps the sole purpose of college admissions was to conduct the most thorough search for students who will leave the campus better than they found it.

After years of never having a choice, hundreds of colleges and universities throw out this golden application for your chance to win a seat at the ultimate decision-making table: our college experience.

But I know you have an analytical mind (you've gotten this far in the book) and you're probably thinking to yourself, after all these news reports, stories, and community anecdotes on the corruption and patterns of ill-mannered influence: **enough is enough.**

So, I ask this question of you: "If you had to describe to four- and five-year-old kids the college admissions process, what would you say?"

Personally, I would start with by telling them that they have around twelve years before this question becomes relevant. Then I would say, "College to most people is a passport into the unknown future. However, college to the real travelers is just the plane ticket to a destination you can create or find yourself." If I were a four-year-old, I would probably just nod my head and ask, "Why?" or "How do you become a real traveler?"

This is where hacking college comes in.

> **DISCLAIMER:** *I am not by any means referring to literally hacking college because it is not a step worth taking, exploring, or considering. You need to play to your strengths in a respectful and honorable way. Those who take college admissions way too seriously like the scandals we've seen from prestigious universities or parents who will do everything and all it takes to get into a school DO NOT demonstrate how to unleash their innovative genius.*

Your impact/memorability, systems of support, and personal rate of return based on your education preference determine whether you have or are about to hack the admissions process.

Hacking college involves the four spheres of influence briefly mentioned above.

The admissions process only considers a few key factors when it comes to whom they want to fill their well-rounded class. When you hear the word "well-rounded," what comes to mind? The definition of "roundness" is the measure of how closely the shape of an object approaches that of a mathematically perfect circle.

When I envision "well-roundedness," I don't see this:

I see this:

Yes, I did just create a "shapeless blob" for the second one.

With the way we've tried to fit the image of perfection on the left, we usually end up looking like the beautifully, imperfect picture on the right. And there is nothing wrong with that.

However, once we start applying to college, we strive to mold the shapeless blob into the left image of what we see as perfection, whether it's through mirroring a peer who got into

Harvard, or a family member who spent their college days at Stanford or Vanderbilt.

But if you told four and five-year-old kids to pick an image to play with (given its ability to come to life), they would likely choose the fun, shapeless blob.

The point? Never attempt rigidity or inflexibility. You are a dynamic human being capable of changing and stretching in different directions.

Even if you did choose the gray circle, remember you already are very much like the gray blob: adorable, still maturing, and confused, but happy to contribute to a place that will be lucky to have you.

**

Morgan Rollins, a high school soccer star who turned into a prosthetic activist, can tell you all about malleability and being receptive to change.

Malleability is the skill of having flexibility toward new environments, ideas, and people.

Rollins studies engineering at Temple University, but didn't ever think that she'd be making prosthetic prototypes and spreading awareness about the value of cost-efficient equipment.

In high school, she endured three surgeries and tons of physical therapy (to a point where she momentarily thought she'd pursue PT as a career). In this pain, she also encountered a love for physics. Her path to college aligned with that of a recruited athlete; however, she still experienced change which ultimately redirected her to found a start-up company and social venture called TemPO— Temple Prosthetics—that is gradually changing the city of Philadelphia.

I strongly believe rejection is just redirection and your divergent path is never going to stay strictly straightforward or go exactly as planned. That's life.

Rollins had her sights on playing soccer for the big leagues. She got accepted to a Division 1 school and even played a few games under those shining stadium lights.

However, after her redirection through an unexpected series of surgeries and hospital visits, her supportive teammates helped her realize that transitioning into a new opportunity (one where she found an undeniable spark) was indeed her next step.

Now, you may call her a warrior, but she told me that during the college process the main thought on her mind was, "How can I angle my education and my knowledge into something that will benefit other people?" This is a great question to ask yourself. Her response was:

- Learn how to tinker.
- "Surround yourself with people who will build you up, not knock you down." Find a group of people who are willing to have the same drive as you to help others.

- Don't box yourself into one skill.
  - Don't be a perfect, gray circle; embrace the shapeless blob your interests tend to be!
  - Rollins had her doubters who said "you can't really make that prosthetic...like you're good at soccer. You don't do science." But "you can't" is just another version of a box. Ignite the "can's" and see where your interest can lead you.
- You are a dynamic human. Be positive and kind to yourself.
- Always ask "why not?"
  - Rollins chose to boldly walk up to her professor in a class of over 300 kids, pitch an idea, and ask, "How do I do this?" She ended up with their support and a research grant of $4,000 to build TemPO.
  - As I said in Chapter 7, she created her own independent study course in high school that led her to what she is interested in now

Rollins' approach toward finding her path can be applied to your life also.

"What does it mean to **you** to tinker? How can you play around with your interests to discover what you go to sleep thinking about? Who is your tribe? Why should you have to stick to one skill set? What's the purpose of what you do?"

— MORGAN ROLLINS

Hacking the college admissions process is a very deep conversation that should be thought about and acted on—not obsessed over.

There isn't anyone quite as knowledgeable of that statement than Antonia Liu, the author of *Hack College Like an Entrepreneur: 40 Surprising Insights from the World's Top Founders.* She is one of my biggest inspirations for writing this book!

In her book, she highlights many insightful paths to making the best out of the undergraduate experience and beyond. I recommend picking up this essential read before going off to college or starting your career.

She creates stories that emphasize a life based on your own creation. Clearly, you aren't at a stage where you can fully recreate the college application process, but perhaps including your own touch will guide you in creative pursuits.

Liu lays out ten deep questions to consider when you're in this monumental stage.[74] I will give you the base level of the questions so you can be intrigued to read the rest of her book to find out even more.

1. Am I everything I could be/want to be? Where's the discrepancy between my current self and my ideal self? What's missing?

---

74 Liu, Antonia. *Hack College Like An Entrepreneur: 40 Surprising Insights from the World's Top Founders.* New Degree Press, 2017.

2. What are my life's three most significant and defining stories? How can I best craft these stories to share with others?
3. Why do I share what I share on social media? To educate, to entertain, to inform? Is it of any value to others?
4. If I had a billion dollars in the bank, what would I do? What are you naturally happy doing?
5. If I were to look at my schedule and how I'm spending my time, would it reflect my values, purpose, and ambitions? If not, why?
6. What's one thing I can do that will dramatically change my life for the better? What will "change the game?"
7. How do I perceive myself? Describe yourself in a short paragraph.
8. What am I doing that is secretly a distraction? What things do I need to eliminate from my schedule to make room for what's necessary?
9. What do I want people to say at my funeral?
10. What makes me come alive?

These questions are essential for finding out who you are. I remember in the few weeks leading up to the month of August, when the portal for college applications opens, I couldn't shake the idea that I needed to know exactly who I was before I poured my heart out to a college.

Liu talks about these questions in her chapter "20 Steps to Know Thyself." I didn't know much about who Deborah Olatunji was then.

I knew she was writing a book about student agency which she had mulled over, worked on, and stretched over the entirety of 2019.

I knew she constantly wanted to fast forward to Decision Day in May to see where all the pieces finally laid out and where God wanted her and her friends to spend the next four years.

I knew hacking the college admissions process meant finally having the opportunity to take a deep breath, a nap, and a road trip across the continental United States for the purposes of discovery, rather than a lengthy college tour. *To just commit.*

I know that the Deborah who writes this now comes alive at the idea of people her age coming to terms with their potential before turning twenty, twenty-five, thirty, and so on. To hack college and the admissions process, *you must hack yourself.*

WHO ARE YOU?

This essential question is aiding me as I search for my value and purpose in the activities that fill my day. When drafting your story of personal purpose, think about what you bring to the table and how you want to use that to change the world.

You can stay true to your impact by knowing who you want to be and having a strong support system as previously discussed in the last chapter. You'll be able to see the return of your investment in the admissions process in the direction, reflection, and intention of your application.

Here's some additional perspective and thought to consider. Jill Madenberg, co-author of *Love the Journey to College: Guidance from an Admissions Consultant and Her Daughter*, says "It is equally important to get over being president of everything. The word *president* is often overrated in the college admissions process. There are literally thousands of *presidents* applying to college from all over the country; from just one school with twenty clubs alone, that's likely twenty presidents, twenty vice presidents, twenty secretaries—you get the point. **Being president is not just special enough—it's your contribution to the club that counts.**"

Your contribution to a school, group, or community will not be measured in your title or how well you can flaunt your resumé.

The best travelers make those titles secondary to the plane ticket and focus instead on creating the most beneficial effect on the other passengers in the plane.

How will you leave the community where you grew up? What will they remember? How do you intend on bettering the lifestyles of the new community you're about to disrupt?

How will your identity help you hack the college admissions process? You have learned a couple of ways through these questions and ideas in Part 2 and it continues with knowing how to utilize the outside world.

TAKEAWAYS & LESSONS:

- Where you attend college (if you choose to go) is not who you will be. Ask yourself *why* you want to go in the first place. Look into your answer closely.
- Your impact/memorability, systems of support, and personal rate of return based on your education preference determine whether you have or are about to hack the admissions process.
- Empower yourself as a shapeless blob. Never accept rigidity.
- Discover the power of redirection and the ability to tinker.
- Your shock value goes beyond the leadership position and into the legacy you will leave behind. Tell them what that legacy looks like and how you will bring it into the campus, develop it into the community, and expand it into the world.

CALL TO ACTION

I challenge you to stop worrying. Promise me that wherever you decide to go to school or work after high school, you will strive to make that community as strong, powerful, creative, intellectual, and thoughtful as you are.

PART 3

HOW TO UTILIZE THE OUTSIDE WORLD

CHAPTER 15

FINDING THE CHAMPION WITHIN

———

"Invest in yourself to the point that it makes someone else want to invest in you."

— SARA BLAKELY

"If you always put limits on everything you do, physical or anything else, it will spread into your work and into your life. There are no limits. There are only plateaus, and you must not stay there, you must go beyond them."

— BRUCE LEE

"Feedback is the breakfast of champions."

— KEN BLANCHARD

Your destiny is greatness.

You're on a cloud—the crowd screams, the time boils down to the very last second, and you finish the game on top of the rumbling chaos, with a grin from ear to ear.

This is what I call the traditional Champion moment.

However, when you imagined yourself in this intense situation, ultimately performing at your best and killing the game, did you call those actions Champion moments?

In high school, being a "champion" is not a common term that gets handed to just anyone. You usually must accomplish a substantial feat on a sports team, academic club, or outside hobby. The path to becoming a champion is accessible to some given their resources, connections, and experience. Champions are not made overnight.

I want to show you there are many areas in your life, like the adrenaline rush I described above, that don't always involve high pressure and intensity. Being a Champion means coming to terms with your successes, big or small, and using the outcome of this recognition to spread positive good through the community.

If you're a basketball star, fantastic. Student athlete nation! I wish I could shoot some consecutive threes. *How can you use your athletic prowess to encourage healthy living and sustainable development in your school or an elementary school nearby?*

If you started your own non-profit, have tax-exemption (501(c)3 license), and are just thriving, that's amazing! *How can you spread your knowledge of leadership and initiation to help existing programs around you to gain traction?*

If you wrote your own book, props to you! *How can you use your experience to expand the efforts to increase literacy rates in your state given the opportunity you had to express and experience the power of your words?*

The use of the word "champion" can influence a person in different ways. From perfect attendance to rising star to smartest kid in the class, any number of phrases could change the way I thought about myself.

What if they didn't think I was smart enough?

What if they didn't think my idea could really land?

What if they realized that I didn't think I could do it?

Undoubtedly, having support from mentors, teachers, and parents is important, but the way you see yourself ultimately affects the investments you make to achieving 110 percent of your goals. Similar to the ideas from Part Two, your mind and your network work together in unleashing genius and finding the champion within.

**

The champion qualities parallel those of an artist, entrepreneur, and an activist.

If you look at how these passions collide, you'll realize they all have one thing in common: a goal to advance change or innovation toward an area where a problem has been identified. They also use the skills they currently possess to help solve the issue they are interested in disrupting. Champions see the issue, highlight what skills they can use to solve it, and learn what they lack to act on their troubleshooting efforts.

These are not the only careers or pathways that can demonstrate the characteristics of a champion.

However, when considering those three, I chose the story of the artist to describe myself.

UNLEASHING ARTIST

The word "artist" itself is largely ambiguous, but for my story of art I usually refer to its role in my life. Ever since age two, my mother prepared me and my twin sister for the expectation that the messages that flowed from our vocal cords were to have intentionality, purpose, and drive.

Now, this may sound like tons of pressure for two five-year-old kids, but that kind of mindset slowly grew into my daily routine. I enjoyed singing and all the awareness it could spread, with heart-touching gospel tunes and captivating play scores. However, the wealth of other art forms at my disposal excited me even more.

Uncomfortable nervousness embraced me whenever I felt like I was taking four strides in the right direction. With three-hour rehearsals, warm-water regimens, and constant overplay of the words I would soon utter in a second tongue with my own style, I was investing in myself and in the moment the investment seemed to pay off.

In the musical community, I always heard about artists who could play seven different instruments, sing perfect pitch on all the octaves, transpose by ear, and compose on the spot. Like, c'mon!

With a bar set so unrealistically high, I wanted to push myself into an art that would create an even larger impact. After going through the recorder, hand chimes, clarinet, violin, viola, digital mix-boards, and piano, I took a step back to consider what the goals were for mastering each instrument and how I would use the knowledge of to influence a community.

That was when I stepped forward and discovered the true power of my voice.

Mastering other instruments was a fine skill but utilizing them meant exercising a different outcome. While adding guitar to my list of musical partners could result in new songs, I knew honing my voice would better satisfy my hunger for impact.

So after going through all these instruments, thinking I didn't have what it took to make a change, I dug into the root of my insecurity by asking myself, *why couldn't I just use my voice to command a room?*

From there, my voice started to go beyond melodies and into meters, venturing into the world of artistic thought as opposed to artistic sound. Poetry became a powerful outlet for me to reach an audience that sat in front of me, but felt farther away in terms of genuine connection, collaboration, and conversation.

Where an unoriginal song couldn't capture the sentiments of my thoughts, curated poetry fit the situation better. Using my voice started with addressing teen issues I knew were serious, like suicide or feelings of loneliness, that I could explore in songs like "Keep Holding On" by Jamie Grace.

But the poems I wrote on these topics were so much more compelling. My words captured the contrast between lyrical finesse and raw dialogue. Singing opened the door, but poetry rose to the platform. Singing was the starting point, but poetry was my launching pad.

**

Excerpt from "Color-Blind"

I remember being younger
beholding the excitement of my childhood days
Prancing around with children of all colors
Completely oblivious to the anomaly of our racial
*   collaboration*
I remember touching the lush green grass and sliding down
The slick surface of a slide that went on to infinity as I
*   chased my friends around fearlessly*

But, most of all, I remember the limitless freedom I had to
    roam around and be free
To watch TV, play board games, and stay up late until it was
    too dark to see
Myself

Friends, this is what childhood used to look like
And as I've grown up, I've seen the shift from blue popsicles
    to bloodshed
Elated children turn to broken, black bodies
Terrific turn to terrifying
And adventure turn into aggravated assault

Our bodies do not belong to us

The dead cannot be recompensed with filthy money traded
    to gun-holding white men who claim their rights by the
    Constitution
Who claim our rights by the Constitution
Who claim our lives by the—
They say the Constitution is color-blind to at least our civil
    liberties
And that all are equal before the law

Our bodies do not belong to us

Jazmine Barnes was only seven-years-old
Driving with her mother and sister on the last road home
A life taken by several shots
Telling me it's the person, not the Glocks
She'll never get to experience the beauty of resistance and
    the pursuit of happiness

Our bodies do not belong to us

This inequality transcends a past of stripped rights,
Stripped clothes,
And mixed babies born out of white infidelity
It indefinitely perpetuates a lifetime of cultural wreckage
Black kings and queens robbed of their mantle
And replaced in the history books
By a white man who got there first
By a white man who said our significance
Was no greater than 3/5ths of a person
Rummaging through stolen property and calling it their own
Disenfranchising societies
Whose generations would have to thrive off loans
Leaning in and leaning out
Treating us like property
Who merely moved across a line
Searching for freedoms
That would take painful generations to find

Color-blindness is not the lack of vision
It's the lack of color recognition
But first I need you to recognize
The visionaries who propelled racial justice forward
Fighting in the midst of stray bullets and constant disorder
The threat of their lives as they push across the border

Our bodies do not belong to us...

**

I started investing in research on topics I had a strong interest in, devouring books and websites like my budding speaking career depended on it. Inspired by Sara Blakely's words on investing in personal growth, I listened to podcasts, watched documentaries, and studied the way great debaters spoke in order to emulate the prowess of their found knowledge.

With examples to look to, I found enjoyment in hearing paced speeches and well-thought-out declarations, which provided evidence of the speaker's personal desire to grow and empower others with their words.

Taking a "risk" by investing time in yourself will feel awkward at first.

The best way to understand this is through the paradox of time. One day, it'll be your first day of freshman year, your first failed pop quiz, and then it'll be your last first day. Amid all this change, you will still have yourself. Even if the friends you started off with aren't the same ones who throw their caps up with you at graduation, you will have created an identity for yourself.

UNLEASHING ENTREPRENEUR

Entrepreneurs take huge risks all the time. We could immediately call it impulsiveness—without examining how they assess their investments or deconstruct how their process contributed to achieving personal aspirations they used to transform their communities—but that would not do them any justice.

Andrew Yu, Texas native and freshman at the University of Pennsylvania, founded the DICE Initiative knowing just that. The DICE Initiative (also known as DICEi) is a "team of young leaders dedicated to working together and taking action within and across our communities in order to improve our communities. Our strategy consists of a focus on relationships, leadership, innovative social ventures, education, and community."[75]

When we spoke over the phone, his immediate revelation about this startup was: "I knew I was doing things I wasn't qualified for."

So then how did he do it?!

As a former Boy Scout and member of the Debate Team, he was exposed to entrepreneurship early. During his freshmen year, he attended a DECA conference, "a career and technical student organization that prepares emerging leaders and entrepreneurs in marketing, finance, hospitality and management."[76] It changed his life.

His team made it to the international competition stage and there he saw how the experience "exposed me to a whole lot of entrepreneurship because I met these other high schoolers who are pursing really cool ideas that I didn't think were within our abilities."

---

75 The DICE Initiative. "Our Beliefs."
76 DECA Inc. "About Page."

"I didn't know that you can start your own business, as a high schooler, and I didn't know that you could actually turn a profit or that there were specific organizations out there to help high schoolers make their passions, their careers."

– ANDREW YU

He also went to a growth-hacking session and learned more about this exciting new field. It takes original ideas and makes them more effective for the market. The practice of entrepreneurship is incredibly intriguing, and I encourage you to check it out!

Before this experience, he thought entrepreneurship was icky considering the manipulation that could be involved. However, after the conference and attending a presentation on growth-hacking, he learned you can use entrepreneurship to make positive change.

Growth hacking is "a process of rapid experimentation across marketing channels and product development to identify the most effective and efficient ways to grow a business. You can use many strategies that you can find in growth hacking to acquire more customers for a lower cost with long term sustainability."[77]

He created the DICE Initiative after watching his other classmates succeed in building interesting science creations. When they would win, they wouldn't do anything with their projects and immediately started thinking what new concept to build for the next year. Andrew saw this as good work and great research going to waste. So, he set out to make a change.

He thought, "If we're going to make something, we might as well try to make more use of the creations. I don't want these [ideas] to go to waste." His incubator does exactly that, and over the course of his time in high school, he and his team helped to mentor over twenty students with their ideas.

On the topic of science fairs, Andrew noted that participation in them has been on the decline. Only 10 million, or 5.5 percent, of the 58.4 million students in the K-12 system engage in them.[78]

Perhaps this is because of the lack of validation they give students with scientific research that is often a one-way street. It is truly incredible when you can advance a field of research but in many cases, the organizations funding the science fairs, like Intel, realized the students weren't the ones doing the projects and winning at the fair didn't necessarily show a desire to continue to innovate.

---

77 Mackie, Mubeen. "Why Is Growth Hacking Important For A Startup?" Thiken.

78 Hill, Rebecca. "The Rise Of Science Fairs (And Why They Matter)." Parentmap.

In the world of entrepreneurship, there are flaws to be addressed, such as the familiar drop-off from a project executed well enough to win. However, you can also learn to have a vision for a future possibility and realize you have the power to create impossibilities.

Isn't that powerful?

Science and entrepreneurship can go together in helping you discover the champion within. But you must promise yourself that **you** will put in the effort to learn how to turn the impossible to the possible, while picking up the tools that will help you inspire others.

UNLEASHING ACTIVIST

Climate change is real and important for our current lives and near futures. Jerome Foster II, an environmentally conscious high school student from Washington, D.C., noticed the problem with the Earth when he was six years old. It started when he heard about "ozone depletion." However, it wasn't in his science class where he learned this, rather it was in an *Avatar* movie. "That's really how I learned about climate change," he says. "The American education system is overdue to start teaching the facts."[79]

When I spoke with Jerome in June, he told me about how earthquakes happen every single day. Specifically, in Oklahoma, as of September 20, 2019, fifty-three in the span of

---

79 First-Arai, Leanna. "This 16-Year-Old Is Taking The School Climate Strike To The U.S. Capitol." *YES! Magazine*, May 24, 2019.

last seven days. During this month, 127 earthquakes with a magnitude of less than 2.2 occurred.[80]

I was floored by the lack of climate knowledge I initially possessed before our conversation. He chose to run for a school board seat for an elementary school in D.C. and "was on that advisory board talking about public policy and the destruction with how sectioned off everything is. That really inspired me to want to run for Congress when I am twenty-five years old."

Jerome is one of many students who participates in the U.S. Youth Climate Strike organization. Before his sophomore year, he didn't even know if striking was really "his thing." However, after interacting with legislators in D.C. and seeing melting icecaps in the Arctic for himself, he knew he had to act.

He marches with the underappreciated but brilliant Autumn Peltier of the Wikwemikong First Nation, the revered Greta Thunberg of Sweden, and astonishing Isra Hirsi of Minnesota—fellow climate activists who are challenging our lawmakers to get uncomfortable with the fact that they aren't taking responsibility or action toward solving the crisis.

I believe that fixing the climate problem is one of the most urgent issues we need to solve, right alongside troubles in the education system. If you aren't educated about it, it's hard to understand the gravity of what is happening. There are

---

80 Volcano Discovery. "Latest Earthquakes In Oklahoma, USA / List And Interactive Map: Past 7 Days."

many unreported instances of climate chaos that no one has shed light on, like what happened in 2019 with the Amazon burning and the numerous earthquakes that happen every day. Take the time to learn more about ways to help and move your state legislators to address these issues.

**

Investing in finding your inner champion starts with the way you see yourself. In my case, I found the champion in me through my interest in becoming an artist and a creator. Andrew is an entrepreneur and a creator. Jerome is an activist and a creator. We are all able to create great tools that can benefit ourselves, our communities, and our planet, but it starts with knowing and having confidence.

It starts with stepping out of your comfort zone and into the knowledge zone where you can begin to "know thyself" through your passions and interests.

It starts with getting behind something and reaching in front of how you can solve the problem.

It starts with joining a community to accomplish goals, set priorities, and use your abilities to make a difference.

TAKEAWAYS & LESSONS:
- In Part Two we talked about learning to tinker or play around and experiment before finding a solution. Now I want you to take risks in those moments of tinkering

and think beyond the original. Don't think, "Why me?" Think, "Why *not* me?"

- High school is not synonymous with limitation, rather it is like *elimination* and **experimentation**. *Eliminate* doubts. **Experiment** possibilities. *Eliminate* comparison. **Experiment** collaboration. *Eliminate* problems. **Experiment** solutions. You can do absolutely anything no matter your age.
  - Writing a book? Yes. Hosting a podcast? Yes. Starting a non-profit modeled after the minds of Silicon Valley? Yes. Interning for your Congresspeople and then pushing them to act now on climate change? Yes. Becoming a paid public speaker? Oh yeah! Tweeting @deb_olatunji about how you've been changing the narrative of what it means to be a high schooler? Done deal.
- None of your ideas are a waste. Say that with me, "None of my ideas are a waste. They all have purpose." All the activities you do expose you to more opportunities to find your inner champion. The ideas you come up with may be the starting point for the change you seek.
- Know the facts. Your ultimate secret weapon is utilizing your environment to come up with solutions to issues. Find credible sources of information on the problem. Educate others to get them informed too.

CALL TO ACTION
I challenge you to find your champion through the activities you do, communities you interact with, and problems you solve. Have a drive toward your passion and learn from those around you.

CHAPTER 16

WHY YOU SHOULD INCLUDE YOUR PARENTS

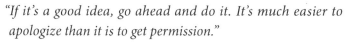

"If it's a good idea, go ahead and do it. It's much easier to apologize than it is to get permission."

— GRACE HOPPER

"The question isn't who's going to let me; it's who's going to stop me."

— AYN RAND

"And the day came when the risk it took to remain tightly closed in a bud was more painful than the risk it took to bloom."

— ANAÏS NIN

From a young age, my mother encouraged me that I was never too young to do anything.

At age four, I started washing dishes and did them so well my mother took pictures of my good work. It was almost as if I knew how to clean so spotlessly from the womb; I could quickly grasp a task reserved for nine- or ten-year-old kids. As a four-year-old, I gave the house a new makeover. My preschool teacher saw the photos and asked if I could come over to do her dishes. My mother and I both laugh at the thought of the fond memory now.

While I never went over to anyone's house with the intent of doing their dishes, my mother's influence shaped my actions and perceptions. As I scrubbed plate to plate, I hadn't thought about the importance of what I was doing; my big brown eyes just lit up at the sight of another object to transform. From dirty to clean, I worked fast.

Both of my parents made the decision to send me to private school for pre-school and late elementary school years, but my mother taught me why I needed to care about my education and my life in the first place.

For ten years, her alarm clock would sound around five a.m., announcing to the world she was ready to begin the schedule for the day. It started with her praying over the school day, waking up my three siblings and me (at the time my little sister was not in school yet), and driving us to Fairwinds Christian School by seven a.m.

She put aside her entire career to raise all five of us—the "O Zone" as we call ourselves. Through her sacrifice, we were able to participate in many activities like theater, chorus, band, and sports. This was the very foundation for the interests that remain with me today. As we learned how to juggle our favorite activities and academics, my mother stressed the idea of being well-rounded and did everything in her power to make sure we were. She would encourage us to get straight A's and wouldn't accept anything less than absolute excellence. As a Nigerian mom, she had her preferences and ways of discipline, but the consensus was that we always did our best, no matter what.

My mother also taught me how to love, how to share, how to talk to God, how to be the one that others would want to follow, how to exercise patience, and how to ask for what I wanted. The anthem she sang to us from our youth was "What you think about is what you bring about. So think big!" In moments where I felt like I couldn't achieve something, like a leading role in a play, a talk with mom would put things back into perspective.

I believe every lesson my mother passed on to us had a purpose. As the saying goes, "When I was older, I would look back and appreciate what she did for us even more."

However, there are a few lessons I didn't learn from her or my dad, that I am seeking to understand as I transition into adulthood. Her complete dedication to making sure we had everything we needed pushed me to work harder for the things that I wanted. Needs and wants were two very different concepts and, as I have grown up, I now know why certain needs must be met before considering wants.

From my parents, I needed five key things: attention, empathy, feedback, encouragement, and dialogue beyond "How was school?" My mother gave me these things in ample quantities, but my father mainly directed his efforts on emphasizing a perfect academic performance. If my grades were suffering, it meant an activity had to be dropped or all of them for a period. Knowing my commitment to these activities, one failure could never surface on my reports. Despite this, my mom supported most of my decisions as long as I kept my priorities straight.

I worked for "good grades" for years because I wanted them and the satisfaction they brought. I participated in many activities simultaneously to build the balance I carried with me into my high school years. From never experiencing failure as a child, I think I caught on to its value much later in life, where it could have helped me to learn sooner.

I want to show you why my mother fulfilling those five needs of attention, empathy, feedback, encouragement, and dialogue were so important in the development of who I am today. Our parents play a vital role in both our education and lives in the journey to finding who we want to become.

**

Here are the five keys to how to include your parents/ caregivers.

ATTENTION

Growing up with five siblings isn't easy; there were days where I felt like I was just another task on the to-do list. What I understand now that I didn't then is how human my mother is. She doesn't have eight arms and two brains to keep track of everything we do. Like most parents, she won't remember a friend's name or what they look like else they come over frequently or come up in our daily conversations. It may take many requests for your parents to pay more attention to your ideas, passions, and wonders. In order to connect with your parents and have them understand you better, you can start by asking them these two questions.

- What is your opinion on the project I am working on? How can I make it better?
- When can we go over the logistics of what I am trying to accomplish? Who in your circle could help me reach my goals?

My project was the summer of 2017. After my freshman year, my older sister exposed my twin sister and me to the large number of summer programs to which we could apply. I searched for programs outside of Delaware and applied before asking if my attendance was a real possibility. Acceptances started rolling in and I created a schedule for my summer to present to my parents. I later apologized for not checking in earlier on whether I could attend. My mother told me that it was better to apply, get in, and then ask, than to not apply and lose the opportunities. Even though I didn't have one hundred percent of her attention on what I sought to achieve, I still included her in the process and showed her my options before solidifying any plans.

EMPATHY

In any education experience, your parents' attention or lack of attention to your academic goals can be either beneficial or detrimental.

It can be beneficial if you need to have a system of accountability, but detrimental if having big goals and getting the grades you want is only for your parents' approval. Let me make this clear: empathy does not equal reliability. The point of accountability is making sure you can get tasks done in a timely manner, but it doesn't mean your parents are doing said tasks for you. When your parents care about what you are investing your time in, they accept being cheerleaders rather than teammates.[81] They can praise your efforts, but cannot do the job for you.

The idea of a parent having too much control over your purpose and desires is a style known as helicopter parenting. In one national survey of college students, thirty-eight percent of freshmen and twenty-nine percent of seniors said their parents intervened on their behalf to solve problems either "very often" or "sometimes."[82]

Helicopter parenting has been said to be the plight of our generation. A parent solving a problem for you is not the same as caring about the steps you are taking to do it yourself.

---

81 University of Delaware Cooperative Extension. "How Parents Can Help Their Kids Be Successful In School." University of Delaware.

82 Almendrala, Anna. "5 Signs You Were Raised By Helicopter Parents." Huffpost.

My mother wisely acknowledged that "Giving birth to a child does not give you the authority to think for someone else. I am opportune to be the vehicle that God used to bring you into the world."

The other part of empathy is love. Taking the time to sit with your parents and share your fears, failures, doubts, hopes, strengths, and wishes can bring you closer. I know no family is perfect, and you may have arguments and challenges, but it is important to have conversations beyond how school is going. This isn't an easy conversation, so if you can't have it with your parents, find another adult in your life whom you can trust and talk to about your thoughts and aspirations.

FEEDBACK

No one likes to hear the word "disappointment" or "disappointed." The truth is many of the first goals we set are to please our parents. From performing well in a piano recital to getting recruited by the best sports team in the country, we all seek our own form of greatness.

The warmth and support I felt from my mother's embrace of my older sister writing a book to motivating me when I started writing my own helped me put my first words on paper—I knew I finally could answer the question "What wakes you up?" from Next Gen Summit Co-Founder, Justin Lafazan's outstanding book, *What Wakes You Up?: Designing Kick-Ass Lives Through Entrepreneurship.* My mother's positive feedback reassured me I was making a good choice. She checked in on my progress from time to time and encouraged me to ask more questions. And then find those answers. My entire outlook on changing the education system has been guided by the fact that my mother constantly engaged with me and kept telling me I could do it: that I was unstoppable.

The Next Gen Summit is "the premier conference for young entrepreneurs. It is an online community platform with thousands of members worldwide, empowering content, digital resources, and community partnerships."[83]

You are in a unique position in your life where what your parents say can fundamentally change your life. You can request this feedback from your parents with these two questions:

- Where does my project need [insert area of concern]?
- What is a resource I can use to find [insert object of search]?

ENCOURAGEMENT

Like the cheerleading idea, your parents can support you best when a goal seems unattainable. You can either reward yourself after reaching a milestone or ask your parents to reward you with a dinner with just you (if you have siblings) or a fun activity, like roller skating together. It's even better if they don't know how to do the activity, so you can motivate them as they learn!

The two different kinds of encouragement, verbal and physical, complement each other. Your parents can support you

---

83   Next Gen. "About - Next Gen Summit."

through heart-to-heart chats or simply drive you to practice, attend your concerts, or buy a T-shirt from your business.

DIALOGUE

One of the biggest things I will miss from living with my parents is their proximity. Of course, you can talk on the phone, FaceTime, or text, but none of those come close to the value of face-to-face interactions. I have so much to learn about my mother beyond her formal name of caregiver and there are many stories which she has begun to share with me as I get older. The time that we have living with our parents as teenagers is vital in discovering who we want to be and where we want life to take us.

Our parents are the ones who can teach critical life skills. For example: how to manage our finances, how to plan for emergencies, how to file the Free Application for Federal Student Aid (FAFSA), and how to take care of ourselves. These responsibilities need to be addressed, especially if your parents don't know how to have the finances conversation simply because they never had it themselves. It's important to see where the learning gaps exist, so you can find another person or program to help you learn.

I opened a savings account and received my first debit card at age fourteen. My mother told me to always save money from birthday gifts and writing contests. Looking back now, I wish I had learned about why saving mattered in the beginning. I knew money didn't grow on trees, but I didn't understand how saving a little over a hundred dollars a month then could have helped me now. I wish I'd learned about interest rates, how to budget, and when spending was okay.

**

The most accurate predictor of academic achievement is not "socioeconomic status or how prestigious a school is that you attend. The best predictor of student success is how your family encourages learning at home and involves themselves in your education."[84]

I cannot count how many books I went through in the sixth grade. All I remember is how much my mother championed a love for reading in all five of us. There was never a shortage of good books to read in the house, but if I wanted to find more selections in a certain genre, she happily drove us to the local library.

According to experts, the definition of parent engagement is "parents and teachers sharing a responsibility to help their children learn, meet, and exceed educational goals. Parental engagement happens when teachers involve parents in school meetings or events, and parents volunteer their support at home and at school."[85]

A parent partnership with your education is a fundamental part of being a student and often helps your teachers too. Our parents can be seen as learning coaches and primary guidance counselors. In many ways, they have a large amount of

---

84   Waterford. "How Parent Involvement Leads To Student Success."
85   Ibid

knowledge to share but don't always know everything. That can be reassuring when it comes to navigating your purpose and using your parents' support as a launchpad instead of a landing strip. The knowledge is out there for you to gain; your parents can help along the way.

As my mother always says, "It is your life. You are the one who will go through the pain, the struggle, and the journey. The best we can do as parents is support you. I can guide and counsel you, but you must make your own decisions. If anything happens, you will bear the consequences of your behavior. I don't have the final say as a parent, only God does."

During my college admissions journey my mother searched for help, specifically with reporting financial aid and reading my essays, from the community. She realized that while she didn't know everything about the process, there were people who could help.

In terms of navigating this process, a language barrier can be a hindrance and source of misunderstanding. A whopping twenty-one percent of U.S. residents speak a language other than English at home.[86] I have a few friends who have told me that their parents don't have the best English, which tends to reduce their ability to help in this crucial time period. But the fact that parents aren't or can't be highly involved doesn't mean they're not supportive.[87] Sometimes what you need is

---

86   Dinan, Stephen. "English isn't main language at home for 21 percent in America." *The Washington Times,* October 6, 2015.

87   ClassTag Team. "How To Reach Parents Who Don't Seem To Care About Education." Classtag.

to find a way to learn *alongside* your parent, so they realize this is a learning experience for both of you.

The role our parents play in our education can make or break the experience. Having the building blocks to a supportive community at home can enhance your view on goal setting, reaching certain aspirations, and acquiring new skills. Granted, our parents have moral responsibilities they should uphold, but every household is different. If education isn't championed in your house, try to find places and people to support you in those five ways. Once the parent/caregiver partnership is in place, we can start asking questions about what school should have taught us to make up for diverse home environments. If we can level the playing field for math standards, why can't we do the same for life skills standards? There are vital skills to learn that you probably haven't or won't learn in school.

TAKEAWAYS & LESSONS:

- Your parents/guardians can be a great resource to you if they know how to help.
- Use these last few years living with your parents to understand who they are beyond "mom" and "dad." If you don't plan on moving out until later, still find time to discuss their experiences over dinner or in small pockets of the day.
- Show your appreciation to your parents/guardians for their help, but also let them know when you prefer independence.
- Utilize your parents' circles to your advantage! Chances are, they may know someone who knows someone who

can connect you to an internship, job, or a long-term opportunity into a field which interests you.

- Create a list of actions your parents/guardians can do to help you learn more about yourself and how you want to make an impact. If they can't help with an item on the list, seek guidance from other adults in your network.

CALL TO ACTION

I challenge you to take the time to sit with your parents and explain to them how you feel about your education. If you could define it, what would you say? Compare your experience to theirs and work together to come up with solution to problems you both may have faced as students.

CHAPTER 17

VITAL TOOLS YOU WON'T LEARN IN SCHOOL

———

"Don't ask yourself what the world needs, ask yourself what makes you come alive. And then go and do that. Because what the world needs is people who are alive."

— HOWARD THURMAN

"Make the kids curious about local issues so they can grow to be global thinkers. Problem-solving is a key approach to getting students to think creatively. It's paramount to have students question their realities and be encouraged to solve problems, fail, and iterate."

— GABRIELLE THOMAS

"Money, like emotions, is something you must control to keep your life on the right track."

— NATASHA MUNSON

I remember taking Driver's Education during my sophomore year, and thinking to myself, *this is probably the most experiential course I will ever take here.*

And I was right. We spent classes studying the laws of the road with the promise we would get to practice the material we were taking notes on. The class was straightforward; we were evaluated on a pass/fail basis.

When it came down to finally driving off on the roads of opportunity, my instructor told me many stories of what motivated students to perform well and understand how to drive in a matter of months. My older brother Samuel told me his teacher told him to pretend he was taking a girl out on a date—*no one wants to date a bad driver.*

My strategy was pretending I was a soccer mom, with four kids in the back, who excitedly clamored about the championship match I was driving them to.

My goal? Arrive alive.

But even with the practical application of how to put a car in motion, I never learned about the hypothetical situations that would become more real as I started to drive. From getting into a life-threatening car accident to popping a tire on the road, the list of things that could go wrong was lengthy. And it didn't help that during my senior year, I ended up in an actual car accident and didn't know what to do.

A year after I completed the course, I made the mistake of leaving my headlights on. (It happens to the best of us.)

My twin sister and I stood in the school parking lot without any idea of how to solve this problem. In that situation, I realized we didn't know how to jump start the dead car, where to get the materials to do so, or who to ask for help. I called my dad, who unfortunately was in New Jersey for the weekend on a military assignment. He told me to ask my driver's ed teachers for assistance. Moved by faith, I walked back toward the school and loudly announced the issue at hand.

"Well, I don't know what to do. I've never had a dead car before!" I exclaimed.

"Call dad, maybe he'll know what to do," Dorcas said.

"You don't think I didn't try that already? He told me to ask Mr. T!" The frustration seeped through my voice.

As I raced down the steps to find a solution, a friend of mine overheard me and stopped, asking me to explain the problem further. I explained the lights were left on, the car wouldn't start, and that I didn't know what to do.

Some would call this luck, but I know it is deeper than that. This was divine. I knew the power of the spoken word from experience and felt as if this friend was a definite Godsend.

She happily exclaimed that she had a jump-start cable and knew how to help.

As she led me to her car, I thought about what would have happened if I hadn't said my frustrations out loud. She had a jump-start cable, a red and black, four-tube garden-hose looking lifesaver, and called her brother over to help.

Dorcas and I watched the trouble they went through to align the front of their car to the front of our car to connect the extended cables. They matched the black and red wires, started the car, and worked magic.

In that moment, I thought about how different this situation would have turned out with lack of our knowledge of what to do. My driver's education taught me how to drive and stressed the importance of being a perfect driver, but it never taught me how to handle an engine gone wrong.

Knowing how to jump-start a car is something that could benefit you directly and your knowledge of how to help could re-ignite the possibilities for someone else's car. Even if you don't have drivers' ed at your school or learned how to drive from your parents instead, these are skills every driver should be equipped with to either help themselves or someone else.

After speaking with over a thousand students and doing research on *Forbes*, High Existence, FreedomSprout, Year On, and Lifehack, I came up with a long list of tools we'll need in our lives, but will never learn in school. The extensive list reminded me of an important African proverb: *a closed mouth does not get fed.* You must get what you need.

One of the main reasons why I wrote this book was because I couldn't sit with the fact that people, myself included, were just waiting for education to change.

But the change we truly need, the change that will empower us to chart our own paths, already lies within.

Since when did school stop us from learning something we wanted to know?

I have broken up the tools you need into four categories and have included some ways to teach yourself the skills needed.

1. Personal Finances
2. Mindset and Thinking
3. Business and Productivity
4. Self-Care and Life Skills

PERSONAL FINANCES

Disclaimer: This is a field your parents should guide you through as we briefly discussed in Chapter 16. However, not everyone has financially aware parents; according to a 2012 study, eighty percent of U.S. adults say they could use help with financial questions.[88] Use these topics as a jumping point to learn the skills together!

How To Budget: Understanding budgeting just means keeping track of your spending, choosing where and what to put

---

88 Bruce, Kalen. "The Need For Children's Financial Education." Freedom Sprout.

money toward in each area of your life, and maintaining the plan.

How Compound Interest Works:

Looking at this chart, do you know what any of it means? *Neither do I.*

Year	Year Deposits	Year Interest	Total Deposits	Total Interest	Balance
1	3,600.00	242.80	3,600.00	242.80	3,842.80
2	3,600.00	730.16	7,200.00	972.96	8,172.96
3	3,600.00	1,279.33	10,800.00	2,252.29	13,052.29
4	3,600.00	1,898.16	14,400.00	4,150.45	18,550.45
5	3,600.00	2,595.46	18,000.00	6,745.91	24,745.91
6	3,600.00	3,381.20	21,600.00	10,127.11	31,727.11
7	3,600.00	4,266.59	25,200.00	14,393.70	39,593.70
8	3,600.00	5,264.27	28,800.00	19,657.97	48,457.97
9	3,600.00	6,388.48	32,400.00	26,046.45	58,446.45
10	3,600.00	7,655.27	36,000.00	33,701.72	69,701.72

89

Compound interest can work against you and for you as Kalen Bruce, founder of MoneyMiniBlog, explains.

How it works for you: Investing from a young age can turn a little into a whole lot. $100 invested at 10% interest (annually) means you will have $110 next year. That means $110 at 10% will turn into $121 the second year, and on and on.

---

89 Bruce, Kalen. "47 Things You Weren't Taught In School (That Our Kids Need To Know)." Freedom Sprout.

How it works against you: A credit card charging a 24% annual percentage rate (APR) will render your minimum payment useless over time. A $150 payment on a $5,000 balance will cost you over $3,000 in interest and take almost 5 years to pay off.[90]

This understanding only scratches the surface of how compound interest can affect you. Around forty percent of adults don't understand the power of compound interest.[91]

These are general conclusions; it's always a good idea to book a sit-down with a professional to discuss the details of your situation.

More personal finance tools:

- **How To Save Money and Invest**
- **How Credit Cards and Student Loans Work**
- **How To Avoid Debt**
- **How Taxes and Insurance Work**
- **How To Keep Track of Your Bills**

These concepts can be explored through TeachBanzai.com, a free website and hub for experiential money learning. Over 30,000 teachers use Banzai, an award-winning financial literacy course, nationwide![92]

---

90   Bruce, Kalen. "15 Finance Terms Children Need To Understand." Freedom Sprout.

91   Ibid

92   Mahan, Lori. "Banzai." *Saratoga Today,* October 12, 2017.

You can also choose to learn how to enhance your personal finance knowledge and manage your money alongside friends. Discover the depths of financial understanding on your own by taking massive open online courses (MOOCs) in finance on free education platforms like Coursera or ALISON. Learn more with money-saving blogs like *20somethingfinance*, *The Billfold*, and *The Financial Diet*.

MINDSET AND THINKING

How To Speed Read = The Power of Audio-books[93]: If you currently drive to school and have a working cellphone, it's easy to swap your daily jam from Coldplay to a good book. You can learn so much from books, though it may feel like there is no time to physically read any. You can eliminate that excuse by listening to an audio version!

- Bill Gates, famous entrepreneur-turned-humanitarian and CEO of Microsoft, reads fifty physical books a year.[94] As a full-time student, I read around ten audio and physical books a year.

- The value of reading personally chosen (or friend recommended) books lies in the lessons and stories you can relate to your everyday life. Here are some of my personal favorites and recent interests to start you off:
  - *Born A Crime: Stories of a South African Childhood* by Trevor Noah

93 Amstrong, Brian. "8 Essential Skills They Didn't Teach You In School." Lifehack.
94 Bariso, Justin. "Bill Gates Follows These 4 Rules To Get The Most From His Reading." *Inc.*, November 21, 2017.

- *Talking to Strangers: What We Should Know About the People We Don't Know* by Malcolm Gladwell
- *Educated* by Tara Westover
- *The Martian* by Andy Weir, read by R. C. Bray

How To Foster Creativity: Start by doing! Create a Mood Board, or collection of magazine clippings, old essays, and menus, to show what draws you in. Try to think differently about music, art, photography, sports, drama, band, science, and consider how to pursue those interests in a new way.

- Another good way to foster creativity is to bore yourself or do nothing for three hours. In the time you spend without technology, friends, or one of those interests, you will be compelled to do something outlandish or unusual.

- You can reflect, write, create a song, build an invention, or come up with your own theories about life.

How To Demonstrate Self-Awareness[95]: Understanding yourself is so, so *vital.* From how you learn and how you think to how you interact with others and how your personality works, being self-aware builds an affirmation in yourself that will help you navigate your career, relationships, and life.

- You can do so by practicing mindfulness, keeping a journal, listening to understand rather than to respond, and

---

95 Zhu, Jessie. 2017. "What Is Self-Awareness And Why Is It Important? [+5 Ways To Increase It]." Positive Psychology.

asking for feedback from others. Podcasts are also an incredible way to learn to how to listen closely and gain insights from many different people. Here are some of my favorite podcasts to get started:
- *Small Consistent Actions* by Sam Demma
- NPR's *How I Built This* with Guy Raz
- *TED Radio Hour* with Guy Raz
- *The TED Interview* by Chris Anderson
- *1619 (New York Times)* by Nikole Hannah-Jones
- *Spectacular Failures* by Lauren Ober
- *The Daily Show with Trevor Noah*: "Ears Edition"

- You can even start your own podcast and invite your friends on for the first episode to have conversations about self-awareness!

How To Be An Entrepreneur: I believe that there is an entrepreneurial spirit to be developed in all of us. When I took the entrepreneurship course, ENTR156: From Ideas to Action with Garry Johnson III, one habit he instilled in me and my peers was keeping an opportunity notebook. In this composition book, we were inspired to write down every invention, thought, product, or business we could think of.

- The core rule of the opportunity notebook is that you cannot cross anything out or erase because every idea, no matter how useless it seems, has its value. This practice encouraged me not only to come up with pointless inventions but also fostered a sense of creativity as I drew mock designs of what I thought the products could look like. Here's an example page of my creations:

SwatMe - portable, reusable, survival fly swatter. Have you ever had a pesky fly bother you? Or even just the insane buzzing getting to or in your ears? *shudder* I was riding the school bus one morning (11/15/17), when a fly seemed to have come in through the window and was trapped. I couldn't fall asleep like I usually do and was tired from an all-nighter. I just wanted to swat that thing! (ILLUSTRATION OF PORTABLE FLY SWATTER)

CatchyIfYouCan - An online business, organization, or company name generator that also makes catchy slogans. (My twin sister and I wanted to start a band, but we could never agree on a band name. I thought it could be "Did Ya Copy That?" but she thought it should be The Twin Duo or something along those lines. We didn't want "Double Trouble" because it was so cliché, or the Olatunji Twins with our last name as our distinguishing factor. I.e. The Merrell Twins, The Martinez Twins, The Dolan Twins and so on.) It's a work-in-progress.

SignMeUp (ASL Support) - interactive sign language platform. An app that has a local volunteering database with the deaf community, learning how to sign, and SIGNabrating the language! I've always wanted to learn how to use sign language and felt bad when I couldn't communicate with a deaf person I saw on a daily basis during the summer and in church.

- There are no rules for where you put these ideas! I ended up transferring mine to a Google Doc so I could legibly read them later but didn't re-draw certain ideas like the SwatMe. I kept my composition notebook and look back through it from time to time. I will be starting another one soon! A good way to stay consistent is to try to create one idea a day on your commute to school or during lunch or before practice.

How To Make and Learn From Mistakes: I think a good deal of us know how to make mistakes, but the learning and reflection part of this process is often overlooked. To learn from a mistake, you can dissect it with these questions: *What happened? Why do I consider this a mistake? How did making the mistake change my view about x? Who can I talk to about this? What impact does this mistake have on my routine?*

- Whenever I make an outrageously foolish mistake, I write it down in my "currents" notebook. The "currents" notebook is just a place where I write down daily insights, interesting quotes, people to connect with, new projects to launch—whatever is currently rolling around in my brain. I don't want to lose those thoughts. For mistakes, I write down who witnessed it, what their reaction was, what my reaction was, how it could have played out differently, and what steps I can take to improve in the future. After doing so, I tell myself I cannot occupy my mind with the mistake anymore because it has passed. Later in the year, I'll look back at my mistakes and chuckle at how terrible they seemed at the time.

How To Be Persistent and Resilient: These two traits will arguably help you through every single area in your life. You can practice persistence by making consistent efforts to achieve or create something and show resilience by learning from the "failed" outcomes of the efforts made.

How To Ask Questions: Stay incredibly curious! Always ask "why?" Question people around you, the government, your favorite sports, authority—all of our lives we've been taught to take things at face value and not go beyond what is immediately obvious. I challenge you to think deeper, to probe, to wander into thoughts that are not skin deep.

Building a strong mindset and thinking skills is fundamental to every current and upcoming stage of your life. By practicing each of these tools with your own routine, you will become the best innovative genius you know. It all starts with the mind.

BUSINESS AND PRODUCTIVITY
How To Work a Keyboard (Properly Write An Email, Code, Create a Website):

- Writing an email seems straightforward but you would be surprised at how pivotal it can be in creating a good first impression. Since the person you are emailing likely has not met you or cannot tell your tone of voice through the computer, it's important you open with a greeting like "Good morning Deborah Olatunji,"; use full sentences, "I wanted to reach out to you in reference to the project you have been working on. How can I help and contribute to redesigning education?" Avoid texting lingo, and sign off warmly with your following, "Kind/Warm regards," "Best," and "Have a good evening."

- Grammarly is your best friend! I use this grammar-checking extension for all the emails I send, papers I write, and messages I respond to. The key to all three of these digital skills is learning how to portray yourself in a professional way and communicating clearly on what you are looking to do.

How To Build A Social Media Presence (Instagram, LinkedIn, Twitter): The easiest way to build a social media presence is to connect with friends and friends of friends. Be wary of people who you don't know if you have a public account. One big lesson I learned from a summer program on posts with your location is that you should never post a photo of your location at the time that you are there. The internet is full of people who love you and people who don't. You do *not* want the wrong people to know your exact whereabouts.

- It would also serve you well to stay positive online, post images your thirty-year-old self would not regret, and use your following as a platform to share your interests. Moreover LinkedIn is a professional networking site that can help you find people across the globe. Most of these individuals have worked on the problems you are trying to solve. Plus, there is no age requirement for the popular networking site; I started my profile when I was fifteen. I also found a mentor through LinkedIn after setting up a conversation to interview him for my book. I saw he had extensive experience in marketing and personal branding, which were two tools I didn't know have much experience with. Your social media is what you make it; I was able to launch my national book tour before my book even came out because of the way I used social media. On that note, use your social media in moderation. You don't have to use every single social site out there. I am mainly active on Instagram, LinkedIn, Twitter, and Facebook from time to time.

How To Sell Yourself or a Product[96]: The secret to success is in knowing how to pitch yourself. "Pitching" is a fundamental practice in entrepreneurship that can be used for job interviews, project proposals, and negotiations. It just means strategically positioning yourself for the role you want.

These strategies from *Forbes*[97] and *Business Insider*[98] will help you out! I added some reflection questions to put these ideas into perspective:

---

96 Breslin, Susannah. "How To Sell Yourself." *Forbes,* June 8, 2012.

97 Ibid.

98 Smith, Jacquelyn. "5 Ways To Sell Yourself In A Job Interview." *Business Insider,* May 11, 2015.

1. **Know your "brand":** What is your purpose, mission, values, and interests? What is the problem you want to solve?
2. **Be a storyteller:** What is your story? Who are the characters in this animated version of who you are?
3. **Know your audience:** Who are you speaking to? What do they value? How do your missions align?
4. **Show don't tell:** Use examples in your stories. Don't just say, "I'm a good leader." Tell me about an instance where things went well or wrong and how you stepped up to control the situation.
5. **It's not you, it's "you":** I don't always feel like a superstar all of the time. There will be days where you don't feel one hundred percent unstoppable. In these moments, all you need to do is think of "you" as a superhero version of yourself. What are your best qualities? How can you show them? Play pretend.
6. **Annoy others:** Circling back to the idea of persistence, "It's not enough to just be. There's too much competition. You need to network, communicate, and engage with people as the "you" you want to be, and you won't get there by hiding."[99] What person hasn't responded to your first connection email? Follow-up with them! What opportunity have you given up on? How can you revive it or redirect your pursuit?
7. **Create a motto:** What is your catchphrase? It can be a combination of your interests and ideas. And it doesn't have to be permanent either; you can change it whenever you want. My current catchphrase is "Let's turn failure into fortitude." You can use your line to conclude interviews, in email correspondences, and conversations.

---

99 Breslin, Susannah. "How To Sell Yourself." *Forbes*, June 8, 2012.

How To Express Your Ideas To a Group (Public Speaking): This is something you can practice with your friends. Pay attention to how you move your hands, what words you constantly repeat, and how well you maintain eye contact. As I have learned from speaking to over 3,000 people at various speaking events, eye contact helps build trust and connection. Talk about your ideas and talk about them often. Get comfortable with hearing the sound of your own voice.

How To Start A Business: Find a problem and a way to solve it! Whether it's food waste, access to menstrual hygiene, or lack of representation, create a social venture or business proposition to eliminate a specific problem. Or join a pre-existing business seeking to accomplish the same goals as you. The best way to learn business is to do business. Go out there and solve!

Your business and productivity skills will be paramount for establishing who you are to fellow professionals or new customers. Most of the ideas listed here deal with how you interact with others because those actions will become a reflection of how you see yourself.

SELF-CARE AND LIFE SKILLS

How To Manage Stress: Whether it was due to a busy test week with at least two tests every day or having an event to attend on every night of the week, I used to feel overwhelmed very easily. I cannot count the number of days that I felt stressed out in school and wish I learned more about mental health hygiene, especially when it comes to stress management. The way I tackled stress was through techniques from the American Psychological Association.

1. Learn how to say **no** by evaluating your priorities.
2. Cultivate social support; talk to someone about the challenges you are going through or worries you may have.
3. Eliminate stressors; look at what is causing your stress.[100] Maybe managing your stress means dropping some responsibilities or asking for help. **Always ask for help when you need guidance or don't understand something.**
4. Seek good nutrition.[101] You must take care of your body by eating healthy foods and staying hydrated. As simple as it sounds, drinking water is a great way to rid your mind of stress. According to health professionals, "Stress can cause dehydration, and dehydration can cause stress. It's a vicious cycle."[102] You can break it by building more water consumption into your day.
5. Relax, meditate, and sleep! In my AP English Language and Composition class, my teacher would always allow us to meditate for five minutes before writing an in-class-essay. With my eyes closed and hands held out flat on the cool surface of my desk, I'd take four deep breaths in and four deep breaths out. This mindfulness practice helped me put away my doubts or worries to free my mind to write.
6. Refocus by getting physically active.

---

100 Thorn, Beverly, et.al. "Healthy Ways To Handle Life's Stressors." American Psychological Association.
101 Ibid
102 Shaw, Gina and Dr. Brunilda Nazario. "Water And Stress Reduction: Sipping Stress Away." WebMD.

7. Invest in a personal watch to help you keep track of your time. Our usage of technology at the wrong times can cause much stress. I have a simple and waterproof digital one, bought online. This will help you eliminate the idea that you must always have your phone on you. By decreasing phone time, you can increase your focus on what matters to you.

8. Reframe your thinking. Life can be stressful, but those moments do pass. They aren't forever. "If you feel yourself spiraling into imagining worst-case scenarios, acknowledge those negative thoughts and then let them ride away. Be realistic with yourself. Accept that some situations are out of your control."[103]

How To Build Real Relationships: Good relationships with your closest friends, peers, teachers, and parents need six things to thrive: trustworthiness, dependability, respect, honesty, patience, and loyalty.[104] You can build relationships with others by communicating your needs and listening for how you can help them thrive alongside you!

How To Do Basic First Aid and Emergency Response: You may have learned about some of these techniques as a freshman but refreshing your mind on how to help someone when they're choking or wounded is important. Always remember to call 911 and administer CPR if they are not breathing.[105]

---

103 Thorn, Beverly, et.al. "Healthy Ways To Handle Life's Stressors." American Psychological Association.

104 Sicinski, Adam. "Six Ideas For How To Build A Loving Relationship." IQ Doodle.

105 American Red Cross. "First Aid Steps | Perform First Aid." Red Cross.

- As accidental deaths due to drug overdoses continue to rise, it is vital to know how to take care of a friend or peer who has overdosed. There are places where you can learn how to administer Narcan, "a nasal spray and antidote to opioid related incidents. It delivers a consistent, concentrated 4 mg dose of naloxone (HCl) that can reverse the effects of a life-threatening opioid overdose in minutes."[106]

- It does not require specialized medical training and "can be found as an OTC (over the counter drug) in most states. You could save a life, but it doesn't replace emergency medical care. You must seek emergency medical help right away after giving the first dose of Narcan, even if the person wakes up."[107]

**

High school is supposed to be the center for exploration, innovation, and collaboration for your future. While it can be frustrating sometimes to think about all the tools you didn't learn, your self-awareness to gain these skills will propel your drive in doing so. Four years is more than enough time to break down all these topics into your personal curriculum; there is still time to gather and refine many of the tools listed into your genius toolbox. Even if you've graduated from high school, it would serve you well to learn these skills.

106 Narcan. "What Is NARCAN® (Naloxone) Nasal Spray." ADAPT Pharma, Inc.
107 Ibid.

TAKEAWAYS & LESSONS:

- Learn how to jump-start your car. Leaving your high beams on is something to be prepared for.
- Take a massive open online course (MOOC) on personal finance during the summer or with friends during the school year.
- Make it a habit to write in your opportunity notebook both useful and "useless" ideas. Draw them out and write about how you could go about turning the idea into action.
- Listen to one or two audiobooks/podcasts this month.
- Talk to others when you are struggling. Building persistence and resilience comes from constant reflection which will aid your stress management. Find outlets for self-expression and self-discovery. Surround yourself with positives. Never forget to take care of yourself, my friend. There is only one you.

CALL TO ACTION

There are even more tools than the twenty-three listed in this chapter that will be vital to your life as a student growing into an adult. **I challenge you to add at least one more tool to each of the four categories. Share it on your social media with the hashtag #vitaltools and #uyigschoolnevertaughtme.**

CHAPTER 18

WHY YOU NEED A MENTOR AND WHERE TO FIND ONE

"Find a group of people who challenge and inspire you, spend a lot of time with them, and it will change your life."

— AMY POEHLER

"If we start being honest about our pain, our anger, and our shortcomings instead of pretending they don't exist, then maybe we'll leave the world a better place than we found it."

— RUSSELL WILSON

"Some of the most comforting words in the universe are 'me too.' That moment when you find out that your struggle is also someone else's struggle, that you're not alone, and that others have been down the same road."

— UNKNOWN

The best opportunities come from the people you haven't even met yet.

During the summer of 2017, the months leading up to my sophomore year, a woman from TeenSHARP reached out to me about an upcoming design sprint for a new startup. They were centered on youth development and wanted high schoolers to be part of the creation stage as soon as possible. That woman was Gabrielle Thomas, the founder of the Delaware Youth Advocacy Council. It was a normal July afternoon; I had nothing to do and not a single reason to say no.

My mother dropped Dorcas and me off at a co-working space called 1313 Innovation. I walked in to see the surrounding glass building that housed the creation of new projects, finished presentations, and freshly prepared Dunkin Donuts coffee. I didn't know anyone or anything about what the day held prior to arriving. But I did know that there would be free pizza. You can never turn that down. I mean unless you're gluten-free.

Zach Jones, the director of the program that would later become Dual School, was joined by the founder of the Summer Learning Collaborative, Catherine Lindroth. She excitedly spoke about education and innovation in a way I had never heard before. In her 2017 TEDx presentation, she advised her middle school audience, "Start now. Because you cannot wait until you are in high school or college or in your career to do this. You have to start now. Because then you would have developed a skillset to light the world on fire. To really bring your ideas and your vision into the world."[108]

Her energy was contagious; however, what was this "now" she was talking about and what kind of skillset lights the world on fire?

Sitting on the edge of a tabletop with a pen stuck in her hair, she bounced around the room asking people for their feedback on what worked in education and what needed to change.

In the two hours we spent brainstorming, we came up with an interactive and engaging alternative for teachers and students to gain more from the education system. In order to test the rough ideas, Catherine had the kids who looked to be around my age or slightly older pair up with an adult in the room. Then, we held model mentorship sessions with our new friends. We were told to talk about a problem that we wanted to solve and how we wanted to pursue the solution.

For me, education was the overarching problem I wanted to solve. At first, I didn't know what my "innovative education project" was supposed to look like. I knew I wanted to talk with someone who understood the current landscape of the system. So, I sat down with Maggie Deptola. At the time she was working as the Chief Operating Officer of Coded by Kids, a local nonprofit that aspires to make technology education accessible to all middle and high school students.

---

108 TEDx Talks. "Defaulting to Yes | Catherine Lindroth | TEDxYouth@ IndependenceSchool." YouTube, Apr 14, 2017.

A key part of having a good mentor was making sure their skillset could help support my development and growth in the field I wanted to redesign.

Over veggie pizza and iced tea, she asked me, "What bothers you?"

"Not much. I just wished school was more interesting," I replied. We had bonded earlier about fitness and track and field. For a real mentorship to succeed, there needs to be a baseline chemistry between a mentor and a mentee.

"How so?" Maggie responded. She ate her salad and looked at me pensively.

"I struggled so much in my freshman math class and I think the issue was in how the lessons were taught. The material wasn't new, but the technique always frustrated me," I said. I tried to block out the memories from that class as hard as I could.

"So Math bothers you then. If you could design your own course, what would it look like?" Maggie pulled out a notebook and wrote stuff down. She was focusing on character rather than my intellect. This was another fundamental element of mentorship. With that one question, she went beyond competency, focusing on helping to shape my character, values, self-awareness, empathy, and capacity for respect.[109]

---

109 Tjan, Anthony. "What The Best Mentors Do." 2017. *Harvard Business Review,* February 27, 2017.

"I guess I would start by asking the students what they wanted to learn." Class participation would have more importance, if we used it in the right way, I had thought to myself. People would want to pay more attention.

"Okay! Then let's map this out. What objectives would you seek to achieve in your own program/startup/course/whatever you want to call it. What is the mission?" She fired away with questions to help me think of a solution; I sat in my chair shocked.

She didn't question whether the problem was with me or my perception of the class. Instead she jumped right into how to make my hypothetical idea work. Never in my life had I experienced a response quite like this from someone I didn't even know. My model mentor listened to what I had to say, asked more questions to guide me to a solution, and didn't undermine my ideas, thoughts, or feelings.

As the hours passed, the topic which bothered me turned into a consulting company. We called it D.E.B.—Dynamic Education Builder. And yes, it was named after me. My mission? I wanted to tackle the lack of engagement in classes and strengthen relationships between students and their teachers. I planned to go into high schools to try to "diagnose" what was wrong with the classroom environment. I also intended on noting cues from students' responses to new material and helping create a more cohesive education delivery system.

All of this from one model mentoring session.

Just one.

And yet, this one experience, this one design sprint, this one conversation, led me to understand the value of having a mentor. A person who listened to what you had to say and encouraged you to pursue your ideas at higher levels. A person who wasn't obligated to care—but did.

I want to show you why mentorship—the practice of receiving guidance from a person of similar interest and higher access to a specific field—is so important and where you can find a mentor of your own. Even though my consulting company never launched, that one conversation two years ago laid down the foundation for my path to loving, exploring, and speaking about education advocacy. It is one of the many reasons why and how I wrote this book.

While I didn't necessarily pick my mentor in this situation, she perfectly displayed some of the good characteristics that make mentors so valuable. As Anthony Tjan, the author of *Good People* said, "Mentorship is all about being 'good people' and having the right 'good people' around us—individuals committed to helping others become fuller versions of who they are."[110]

**

Dorcas has journeyed with me in our individual pursuits to blossom as young women. I have experienced many life lessons with her. Among those lessons, we constantly faced what I call "eternal comparison," but we discovered how to live our lives without always competing.

---

110 Ibid

Ever since we were little people have found various avenues to lift one of us, while belittling the other's potential.

We just couldn't win. Not at the same time, at least. From day one, August 14, 2002, it would become common practice for people to compare my pineapples to her strawberries and try to make them resemble each other as much as possible.

Despite the constant comparison and illusion of absolute sameness, I believe we have our different interests to occupy our days, problems to solve in the community, and innovative ideas for societal change. I want a career in healthcare and education; she wants one in law, business, and education.

Note to self: Don't measure your progress using someone else's ruler. Comparing yourself to another person can make you feel like your process is inefficient or lacking or not good enough. When you spend all that time doubting yourself, you lose sight of the growth you need to become the best version of you.

This is where mentorship complimented my mother's parenting. She did her best in trying to support our ideas and motivate us, but we were still two very different people who each had a wide variety of interests.

During our sophomore year, we both started seeing the value of reaching out to people older than us for guidance. Miracle, our older sister, was a great person to talk to for advice, but the thought of a total stranger replicating that same curiosity and attention toward my life seemed interesting and different.

Dorcas' first mentors came from Dual School, a student-idea incubator in Wilmington, Delaware's entrepreneurial hub. She engaged in a community that changed her perspective of education. In each of the ten Tuesday afternoon sessions, she worked with the program's diverse cohort of high school students from public, private, charter, and vocational schooling.

After choosing a problem or topic to solve and explore, she created a team of adults who were connected to the solution she wanted to find. Through rapid prototyping, designing surveys to assess the problem, and weekly check-ins on her progress, Dorcas found ways to make this new learning practice work for her.

She experimented with entrepreneurship in many ways. At her first pitch competition, she talked about creating a carpooling application geared towards increasing the accessibility of opportunities for students who lived far away from school. She pitched the idea t^2, which stands for transforming transportation, and secured connections with organizations like Great Dames, TrafficCast, and Zipcode Wilmington.

**

According to First Round's study of one hundred mentor/mentee pairs, there are some crucial questions you need to ask in forming a mentorship:[111]

---

111 First Round. "We Studied 100 Mentor-Mentee Matches — Here's What Makes Mentorship Work."

1. Does this potential mentor remember key details about me?
2. Will it be hard to explain the concepts or context of my interest area?
3. Can this person give actionable advice?
4. Does this person seem present and focused?
5. To yourself: *What's that one thing in your path that you want to overcome or achieve to get to a different level in your career?*

You don't have to look very far to find a mentor, but you do want to make sure you ask someone five to ten years older than you, well-versed in relevant career knowledge, and willing and flexible to make a relationship work for the both of you.[112]

**

The TrafficCast pitch competition was forty minutes away from where we live, but that didn't stop her from asking my dad to make the drive up to Philadelphia. It was June, the summer before our junior year. Dorcas walked into the room as the only high school student and away from an audience of stunned adults with the third-place prize of $1,000.

Since we were both busy and out-of-district students without drivers' licenses, Dorcas knew the importance of being able to commute from one opportunity to the next. Her goal was making a platform for students and parents to carpool together from different schools in the same area, but she

---

112 Ibid.

started with one school community at a time. After her insights from Dual School and researching online, she built many prototypes of t^2 and tested them on sports teams in the spring of 2019.

"I wanted to create a database of people with carpooling needs who would benefit from my idea, t^2. I hypothesized using an algorithm or some form of smart technology that could be used to easily match people and create a more efficient community."

– DORCAS OLATUNJI.[113]

I watched Dorcas' journey unfold from the start of an idea to her goal of gaining funding for its launch as an official program. Countless phone calls, video meetings, and full notepads could tell the story of her progress better than I could with my own eyes. The mentors who supported her in conversation, advice, and encouragement helped propel her to the next level. While she is no longer working on t^2, she still carries the experiences, both the successes and failures, on to her next entrepreneurial pursuits.

**

113 Olatunji, Dorcas. "A Teen's Tribute To The Delaware Orgs Guiding Her Along The Startup Path." *Technical.ly Delaware*, August 29, 2019.

The interesting part of mentorship lies in its ample quantity. There are 242,620,800 people in the age range of eighteen to sixty-five plus in the United States.[114] You have much higher odds of having a mentor than an identical twin. That's thousands of education activists, innovators, athletes, CEOs, entrepreneurs, engineers, technologists, artists, and more that you could potentially learn from. In the world, there are almost eight billion people and counting.

If I asked you to name five people from whom you could get solid advice and help, other than your family members, whom would you name?

Are you drawing a blank? Stuck on person two or three? That's all right. Dorcas and I brainstormed together and came up with an activity to help you find the answer to this question.

Put your palm out in front of you. Take the index finger of your other hand to draw a circle in that palm. This is your circle of community. Your fingers and thumb represent the five people you should have in your circle.

THE GUIDANCE COUNSELOR: *YOUR PINKY*
This person does not necessarily have to be your school counselor. Their main role is being someone you can talk to for academic advice, whether that be high school or college. With this person, you will want to set up a time weekly or biweekly to discuss your latest ideas, struggles, and stories. You can find a guidance counselor in a close teacher,

---

114 Kaiser Family Foundation. "Population Distribution By Age."

community leader, or relative. This should be someone who values your academics and wants to help you see the bigger picture behind why we learn to begin with.

THE GOVERNMENT OFFICIAL: *YOUR RING FINGER*
This person holds a position of power—or any kind of legislative position where they have connections—that connect you to other people in the formal decision-making sphere. The reason you need them in your circle is to acknowledge the changes happening in your problem of interest and propose your own unique ways to solve them. If you engage with people on the school board, the Board of Directors of your place of worship, or your State Board, you are positioning yourself to learn what their powers mean and how they can benefit the community.

I recently found an interest in menstrual health advocacy and started working with my State Senator Tizzy Lockman to create more access for women without these essential rights in Delaware and in our high schools. She is working with Delaware House Majority Leader Valerie Longhurst to introduce legislation for middle and high schools and charter schools to provide free feminine hygiene products.[115] A friend of mine, Nabiha Syed, organized a rally in October during the first national period day led by Founder and Executive Director of the non-profit organization PERIOD, Nadya Okamoto. The goal is to curb the stigma around menstruation. At the Delaware rally, I marched with Tizzy, chanted protests, and spoke on period poverty through a poem. This experience

---

115 Mueller, Sarah. "State Lawmakers Plan To Require Schools To Provide Students Free Sanitary Products." *Delaware Public Media*, October 18, 2019.

showed me the power of assembling with people of common interest to make a statement and demand action on the change we seek.

THE LIFE MENTOR: *YOUR MIDDLE FINGER*
This person does exactly what the title sounds like; they help you assess your priorities and determine how to maintain a balance in your life. You can think of them as a parental figure, but at the end of the day you choose what to share and what not to share. It can even be your parent! They do more than just tell you ways to live your life by allowing you to make the decisions and ask for advice from there. This role tends to overlap into the other parts of the circle, which is okay if this person is interested in maintaining communication with you and building a relationship that encourages self-awareness and respect.

THE BEST COMPETITOR: *YOUR POINTER FINGER*
Can you guess who my best competitor is?

Yup! It's Dorcas.

The aspect of competition is very different from comparison in how it allows for both "players" to learn from their own mistakes and those of their friend. This person should be someone your age who keeps you on your toes and pushes you to think creatively. They inspire you to never be satisfied with a linear pursuit of success. Dorcas and I do this with a monthly opportunity log where we document what we applied to and when the application was due. We refer to the log as Application Ninja, a concept from TeenSHARP, that cultivates a spirit of friendly competition while exposing both parties to ongoing opportunities for which the other person is reaching.

The number of opportunities relate to a specific belt color. Four opportunities are a yellow belt, seven is an orange belt, ten is a blue belt, thirteen is a green belt, seventeen is a brown belt, twenty-one is a black belt, and twenty-five opportunities and beyond is the red master belt.

I never found it beneficial to keep good opportunities away from my sister, and by using AppNinja, we motivate each other to meet deadlines and apply to more experiences. You want to pick someone who will genuinely be happy and excited about your success and be a player who seeks to lift them up and celebrate them as well. As Adam Alpert, Co-Founder of Pangea.app, says, "Open doors for others and give thanks when someone else opens one for you."

THE NOTEBOOK: *YOUR THUMB*

The last person is your notebook or genius pad. You need something to vent in because your mental health is important, and this practice of daily writing will help you become more conscious of yourself and present in the moment. Experts estimate that the mind thinks between 60,000–80,000 thoughts a day; that's an average of 2,500–3,300 thoughts per hour.[116]

---

116 Sasson, Remez. "How Many Thoughts Does Your Mind Think In One Hour?" Success Consciousness.

Isn't that cool? You need a place to put those thoughts down. It's also good to have somewhere to keep track of your accomplishments, reminders, and personal notes: where your thoughts go to play.

These elements of the community circle tend to shift and change as you learn more and experience more about what you want to see change in the community. It is a circle because these people are in your reach, but you don't have to be in contact with them all the time. The comfort of knowing they are there whenever you need to connect with them builds a sense of community, connection, and contribution to improving the situations you find compelling.

**

In high school, the people you surround yourself with tend to dictate your outlook on the situation. If you surround yourself with people who are not motivated, hate school, or have no desire to learn beyond the curriculum, it can be difficult to develop your own strong sense of self-awareness. By having a circle of people and toolbox of skills to understand who you are, you will be taking the right steps toward unleashing genius. Mentors share their expertise with a consultant mindset, guide you along your journey, without giving away all the answers, and become cheerleaders when you need it most.[117] Those traits are invaluable and once you have found these people to grow with, then you have hacked *life*.

---

117 Wright, Michelle. "The Three C's Of Mentorship." Ye!.

TAKEAWAYS & LESSONS:

- You can have more than one mentor. Sometimes you can have a whole team! Find people to whom you can relate on a personal and professional level. The chemistry must be there as well!
- Do not, I repeat, DO NOT measure your progress using someone else's ruler. You are destined for your own kind of greatness.
- Your circle of community, the guidance counselor, the government official, the life mentor, the best competitor, and the notebook, can help you learn more about yourself and the impact you want to make.
- Seek opportunities and ways to connect with your community. Once you have found your circle, help a friend find theirs! Create #geniuscircles all around you.

CALL TO ACTION

I challenge you to write down the names of the people in your circle of community on your hand. Put your name in the center of your palm. Take a picture of your entire hand and post it on LinkedIn, Twitter, or Instagram with #uyig-circle and tag me and the people on your fingers! Check out mine and more resources at deboraholatunji.com!

CONCLUSION

HACK LIFE! UNLEASHING GENIUS

———

Sparked ideas—the ignited embers within us that lead to further self inquiry; the brush of light when a stray thought turns into a life-changing movement.

You will have these moments of light, energy, and inspiration. Days where your ideas are the currency of innovation and ambition, the incentive that drives you to want more.

More creativity.

More community.

More connection.

More influence.

This is what we can do in today's school environment and outside of it when we work together.

**

I have learned more from doing things outside, rather than inside, the classroom.

Even though I am less than two decades old, I know this coming decade must be altered to help propel future generations. The change I seek will not come in a lone effort to persuade my state policy makers or even write this book. Yes, it will help, but in order to fully mobilize the children of the broken education system with the tools needed, we collectively must work together to redesign traditional methods. We must create a framework that allows for our own personal development.

As the CEO of GripTape, Mark Murphy, said to me, "If schools in this country got significantly better at providing kids with foundational knowledge accompanied with real competencies and deep understandings, then together they could transform education." This transformation requires our input as students who need to experience this foundational knowledge.

I see an education system in our near future where identity and agency go hand in hand. In this way the stories we take with us will inspire other generations to continue to innovate.

When considering how to take control over your high school experience, start by asking yourself these questions:

- Who am I?
- What do I value and care about?

- What problem do I want to solve?
- What solutions do I want to build on for the good of my community?
- Whom can I ask for help?

Many people, even those outside of education, believe:

- Students don't know what they want in the education system and are happily going through it without resistance.
- Teenagers are too inexperienced to know what changes need to happen and how to enact them.
- The school system is the exact same way it was when they left over ten years ago and if it needs a fix, it will fix itself.
- Educating young people doesn't require change—the traditional model of education is working.

I believe those assumptions are false. When students understand why they need to create their own access and where to find systems of support for the cultivation of their ideas, real change happens.

Many people, even those outside of education, **need to see**:

- Students DO know what they want in the education system.
- Teenagers are HAVE THE EXPERIENCE to know what changes need to happen and how to make those changes happen.
- The school system IS NOT the same way that it was when they left over ten years ago and not only does it need fixing; it WILL NOT fix itself.

- Educating young people DOES require change and the traditional model of education IS NOT working.

The goal of education should be growing more creative student leaders and innovators, instead of creating robots who act the same, think the same, and ideate the same.

However, by redesigning your education experience, you can *unleash your innovative genius.*

FEATURED POEMS

Here are the full length versions of the poems mentioned in Chapters 15 and 18. I encourage you to find your own path in poetry, whether you love writing, like reading, enjoy watching, or savor listening to these vulnerable pieces of yourself or someone else. You never know how far one piece will take you.

All the best,

Deb

**

COLOR-BLIND

BY DEBORAH OLATUNJI
January 20, 2019

I remember being younger
beholding the excitement of my childhood days
Prancing around with children of all colors

Completely oblivious to the anomaly of our racial
    collaboration
I remember touching the lush green grass and sliding
    down
The slick surface of a slide that went on to infinity as I
    chased my friends around fearlessly

But, most of all, I remember the limitless freedom I had to
    roam around and be free
To watch TV, play board games, and stay up late until it
    was too dark to see
Myself

Friends, this is what childhood used to look like
And as I've grown up, I've seen the shift from blue
    popsicles to bloodshed
Elated children turn to broken, black bodies
Terrific turn to terrifying
And adventure turn into aggravated assault

Our bodies do not belong to us

The dead cannot be recompensed with filthy money traded
    to gun-holding white men who claim *their rights* by the
    Constitution
Who claim *our rights* by the Constitution
Who claim *our lives* by the—
They say the Constitution is color-blind to at least our civil
    liberties
And that all are equal before the law

Our bodies do not belong to us

Jazmine Barnes was only seven-years-old
Driving with her mother and sister on the last road home
A life taken by several shots
Telling me it's the person, not the Glocks
She'll never get to experience the beauty of resistance and
    the pursuit of happiness

Our bodies do not belong to us

This inequality transcends a past of stripped rights,
Stripped clothes,
And mixed babies born out of white infidelity
It indefinitely perpetuates a lifetime of cultural wreckage
Black kings and queens robbed of their mantle
And replaced in the history books
By a white man who got there first
By a white man who said our significance—
Was no greater than 3/5ths of a person
Rummaging through stolen property and calling it their
    own
Disenfranchising societies
Whose generations would have to thrive off loans
Leaning in and leaning out
Treating us like property
Who merely moved across a line
Searching for freedoms
That would take painful decades to find

Color-blindness is not the lack of vision
It's the lack of color recognition
But first I need you to recognize
The visionaries who propelled racial justice forward

Fighting amid stray bullets and constant disorder
The threat of their lives as they push across the border

Our bodies do not belong to us

But Martin Luther King, Jr. poured into a melting pot of
public outrage and resistance
Leading a strong, unbridled congregation who marched to
Memphis with persistence
He saw a Promised Land in the midst of dry bones and
white aggression
From segregated bathrooms to white men "tryna teach
Emmett Till a lesson"

And despite all this
He left a legacy of non-violent progression
Facing arrest, bomb-threats, and personal abuse
We glean that our words and action must be put to CIVIL
use
With innocent blood smeared on *their* hands, whips on our
backs, and tears in our eyes

Our road less traveled leads back from a lost prize
To sitting and sleeping in a library and someone calling
the cops
To walking by the cornerstone and almost getting shot
To tossing misidentified bodies into the suffocating sea of
black oppression
"We may have all come on different ships, but we're in the
same boat now"

Our bodies do not belong to us

People tend to forget that the legacies of persistent
    individuals
Will not die at the barrel of their guiltless guns
The power of our change cannot be deterred
The strength of our Dream will not be deferred
And *the unity of this community* shall withstand the
    collective collaboration of killing our people

King dreamed and dreamed, and that dream could not be
    thwarted
He taught us to persevere and press until something
    happens
Push until something breaks

This isn't just about race relations
This is about the human civilization resorting to things
    that are not even civil
Restricting access to opportunity and calling us equal
Great, proud, home of the free
Home of a nation that rose from the bedrock of slavery
Home of the ones who will see my color before they hear
    my words
Home of the ones who killed Eric, Trayvon, Philando, and
    Freddie
Them and more buried in the bosom of **black history**

Our bodies do not belong to us

The violence that consumes us is almost twice the size of
    our population
Does not happen anywhere else but this "united" nation
Do not get me wrong

Being color-blind does not mean being neutral to *our* past
pain and neutral to our current needs

It is not *assassinating* Martin because he had a family to
feed

Being color-blind does not mean letting people walk all
over you and take what is yours

It is responding to life's most persistent and urgent
question, **"What are you doing for others?"**

It is remembering to not forget the importance of my own
history

Because white children get representation in my education

And I am left picking up the broken pieces and filling in
the missing blanks on my own

The other day a classmate of mine forgot who Harriet
Tubman was

As if her legacy was not significant enough to come across
his white-washed recollection

Reminding me that they cannot find the answers to my
questions

Can't we be color-blind to our physical features and rather

Observant of the greatness of our legacies

She set millions free

And as King affirmed "One day my four little children will
live in a nation where they will

Not be judged only by the color of their skin

But by the content of their character"

We, as 5/5th's of human beings, are entitled to *our*
freedoms and *our* social, economic dreams

"And I will not apologize for being outraged because these
times are outrageous"

If 1968 was the color-blind dream that I see
Then the prospect of black prosperity would no longer rest
    on the crux of white shoulders
I'd see the pigments of injustice transforming into vivid
    hues of unity
And Martin Luther King, Jr. smiling proudly over that
    cold, April balcony
The world would be a different place where freedom reigns
    and people sing
We can all live together in a world that sees my character
    for me
We can see the dream being fulfilled with 51 great years of
    racial and economic peace
We can all live together in a society that truly proclaims
    the fundamental rights of human beings
I remember being younger
beholding the excitement of my childhood days
Prancing around with children of all colors
Completely oblivious to the anomaly of our racial
    collaboration
Friendships in a world that let us all be
Color-blind

**

TO BE WOMAN IS TO BE HUMAN

BY DEBORAH OLATUNJI
October 19, 2019

What are the basic human rights of a society so consumed
    by the concept of freedom?

A country emboldened enough to make little girls and
little boys recite their promise of liberty before basic
arithmetic in the morning, disregarding the freedoms
it had already stripped away

Test today

To be student is to study
To be student is to learn
To be boy is to play reckless and unapologetically demand
for more and more
Taking and taking and taking

The division of power requires someone else to give up
theirs
Whether willingly or unwillingly willpower whisked away
To give up pieces of their freedom
To give up places on their platform

To be woman is to be human
From the very first drop that society deemed us female
From every tear-jerking rom-com that told us we were
damsels in distress
That needed someone
Or something
To give us the power
we need to be we.

To be woman is to be human
From the very first splotch of our life-bringing ability
We heard of periods

But never spoke of their power as if saying the word alone
        could transform us from
The carriage into the pumpkin
that we knew we'd later become
Not realizing that this story, this fight, this rally, this
        protest, this demand for what it necessary not
        an option,
Is not a fairy tale
And does not need magic
We need action
Woman

With this "painless" knowledge and confirmed truth
Biases and judgments that would follow through our youth

Our womanness did not start with the number of eighteen
But rather the end of a sentence that was really just the
        beginning
Period
Period power couldn't be shared because they will never
        know what it is like
To call out sick and really be sick but still sickly arrive to
        school, work, church, gym
Having 3-7 days of pure torture only to be reminded that
        our pain could be interpreted otherwise
"You're not yourself today"

Hmmm
I wonder why
Because my uterus is sending messages in Morse code that
        can't wait 'til next period
Period

I'm telling you through tears that this isn't something that
    just goes away
It lingers for more than just today
And then shows up to surprise me
To remind me
That I am still woman
And you tell me that I am not myself today
Well maybe it's time you thought about what it meant to be
    me in the first place

Listen
What about period poverty
Black women make 68 cents to the white man's dollar
Latinas with as low as 42
Those are some short facts but when you do the research
It adds so much more urgency

So, what can we do?

Let's stop making womanhood
something we have to hide
Like bringing forth life is a forbidden secret
A story never shared, and a baby never had
Because pink tax and race deductibles are so real here
Because your physical appearance shows you just how
    privileged you are

And the fact that you can't look me in the face and say
    menstruation
Or period
Or tampon
Or pad

Or bleeding
Or blood
Or the majestic nature of life
Is insulting
And I will no longer let your ignorance serve as our
    punishment
Your naive nature passing us by

This period does not mean an end
It means that we as women can begin again
And the moment we stop making the essence of
    womanhood a luxury afforded only
To those we deem worthy
Then we can authentically say that to be woman is to be
    human
And this movement is a human right.

Period.

ACKNOWLEDGEMENTS

Unleashing Your Innovative Genius would not have been possible without the following people. I am grateful for each and every single person and experience that led to its creation—I could not have written this book without them.

I want to thank God for His grace and for blessing me with such an introspective group of individuals. Thank you to my parents and siblings (Samuel, Miracle, Dorcas, and Testimony) for always been there. Thank you for being my first community and soundboard to talk to about current events, differing ideas, and hopes for the future.

Thank you to all of the students who contributed to these stories through dialogues, social media, summer programs, and classrooms. The time that I spent with all of you showed me that my struggles with education were not personal problems, but global ones. Thank you for having a conversation with me, for laughing with me, for growing with me, and for learning with me. Thank you for understanding the power of being sure of yourselves and being able to live a life beyond academics. I know that you are all truly unstoppable; our interactions changed my world for the better. For those of you I have not met yet, thank you for your time, attention, and mind. Without you as a reader, this movement cannot happen.

I would not be the person I am today without all of the summer experiences that led me to discover the importance of conversation and experiential learning. These programs shaped and honed my thinking, personal development, approach to networking, communication, and self-awareness. Thank you to the staff and students at the Economics For Leaders Program, ACLU Summer Advocacy Institute, the University of Delaware's College of Health Sciences Summer Camp, the American Legion Auxiliary Girls State Program, the University of Pennsylvania's Kelly Writers House Workshop, Northeastern University's Bioengineering Immersion Program, and the Distinguished Young Women of Delaware Program.

To my Economics For Leaders family, thank you for being the first group of high schoolers that I became friends with outside of my little Delaware. I didn't even know that Ohio or Wisconsin existed before the summer of 2018! This summer program—the first one that I ever applied to—taught me how important diverse voices are in the international market and in the game of life. Thank you, Izzy, Kristyn, Ben, Diana, Drishti, Yejide, Omar, Sonit, Kye, Jonathan, Samir, Carlos, Jarrett, Riley, Jeffrey, Tim, Giuliet, Layla, Wendy, Leslie, Alessandra, Jane, Evan, and Elias for teaching me how to take risks, to be vulnerable and open in front of strangers, and to put a party together in less than six hours. You were all instrumental in the creation of the person I have become today and will be tomorrow.

Thank you to my GripTape family: Mark, Catherine, Amy, Annette, Danyelle, Mahika, Austin, Kimani, Maggie, Madison, Bemnet, Megan, Abi, Landon, Alyssia Janee, Tasha, Nate, and Kaitlyn, for introducing me to a powerhouse of unstoppable youth. Thank you for giving me the opportunity to take action with education advocacy and see students' lives change right before my own eyes with the power of experiential and personalized learning.

Thank you to Olivia, Britney, Smrithi, Ines, Neal, Farah, Addie, Savera, Kelsey, and Isabel for helping me endure through the beginning stages of my pre-sale campaign and the production of the campaign video during Northeastern's BioE program. The surprises and hope that you gave me on days where I didn't believe in myself and felt overwhelmed by summer work and the book mean the world to me.

Thank you to all of my mentors, especially Rich Keller, for motivating me and listening to my ideas. With your guidance, I was able to start my book tour before the book even launched! That leads me to Penncrest High School. Thank you so much to the Penncrest community for being the first high school to me share my message with you and allow this conversation to officially start! All 1,200+ of you are going to do amazing things and I can't wait to see how you will unleash your innovative genius. To Principal Harrison and Mrs. Somani, thank you for demonstrating why collaborations with students and educators matters. I hope to see more students take their stage, rather than a seat.

Thank you to the Charter School of Wilmington for being my place of growth for four years. Thank you for showing me why learning must happen outside of the classroom as much as inside it. A very special thanks to my AP English Language teacher, Mrs. Hollstein, for joining the list of Advanced Readers and teaching me the mechanics of words. Thank you for your hugs and constant encouragement in this book-writing process.

I am deeply grateful for the people who agreed to let me interview them and for lending me their stories in this book. Without our discussions, the book could not reflect the reality that all of our educational experiences are different in many ways and in that divergence lies extraordinary beauty.

Thank you to my amazing team at the Creator Institute and New Degree Press for accepting my proposal to become a real book. To Eric Koester—thank you for believing in the potential of high school students and creating an opportunity for our voices to be heard.

To Brian Bies, the head of publishing, your dedication to assisting in the pursuit to create creators is unmatched. Thank you for your patience and guidance.

My all-star editors are key players in the creation of this book. To Elissa, my developmental editor, thank you for being my first outside soundboard. I didn't realize how vulnerable writing a book could be until I heard fellow authors talking about it. You gave me confidence in my work from the very beginning. To Maylon, my marketing editor, thank you for being such a down-to-earth, kind, and animated person to work with as this movement went from first draft manuscript to first book. To Gina, my copy editor, thank you for reviewing my final manuscript. The words you gave me when I received my edited manuscript just in time for Christmas will forever stay with me: "Changing the education system is a worthwhile goal, but one that will take time. Metaphorically, you cannot turn a ship on a dime, as it takes time to shift the momentum, but the shift can occur; especially if you have the foresight to see where you want to go and take corrective action when you see you are going to miss the mark. Yet, even after missing the mark, you can still adjust and redirect." How insightful and powerful.

And to everyone behind the scenes, your work does not go unnoticed. Thank you so much.

Finally, thank you to the people who pre-ordered the eBook, paperback, multiple copies, and donated to make publishing possible! Thank you for spreading the word about *Unleashing Your Innovative Genius* and helping me publish my first book. I am immensely grateful for your support.

Mei Huang
Kimani Calliste
Samuel Olatunji
Richard Keller
Smrithi Dhananjaya
Elroy Huels
Brianne Hane
Kim Lopez
Adegoke Odina
Hannah Ye

Dorcas Olatunji
Shriya Boyapati
Kari White
Michelle Morin
Danyelle Murray
Ralph A Kemmerlin
Donna Urban
Julie Rumschlag
Anthony Papol
Marco Ortega

Brett Levy
Christian van Amerongen
Andrew Avila
Kanyia Charles
Gemma Hong
Tobi Park
Kelly Eskew
Greta Romano
Zachary Jones
Charles Horn
Paris Gramann
Julia Bacci
Yasmine Signey
Britney Urrutia
TaLisa J. Carter, Ph.D.
Surinder Sharma
Talia Moine
Douglas Kohl
Jenna Sharkawy
Bett Alter
Gerald Larson
Nibedita Mohanty
Julie Frieswyk
Xuan Bui
Charles Munson
Maria Fiscella
Aimee Parker
Morgan Rollins
Raenah Lindsey
Kate Plows
Wyatt Patterson
Mark Ware

Luke Mathe
Morgan Klug
Esther Olatunji
Addie Hegde
James Edwards
Amber Moody
Samson Gelfand
Griffen Ewing
Lisa Penfield
Maya Birchett
Nomita Patel
Catherine Holland
David Marchino
Grayson Winchester
Lila Feldmann
Anisha Mahuli
Natasha Taylor
Timothy William Marvin Jr.
AaronRey G. Ebreo
Dariya Baizhigitova
Mikayla Dolo-Pittman
Andres J. Martinez
Joan Sharp
Jordan C. Lee
Sophia Block
Savera Hunsberger
Miracle Olatunji
Colleen Degnan
Rebecca Stacey
Angeline Rivello
Jacquelyn Janocha
Maddy Barket

James Massaquoi   Olivia Hadley
Eric Koester   Charleen Chavez

A special thanks to the people and organizations who bought multiple copies or made multiple campaign contributions:

Neal Mehta   **Oladayo Odina**
Linda Underhill   **Lauren Fritz-Mariner**
Penncrest High School   **Simon Youth Academy**

This is the beginning of a movement. Thank you, everyone, for joining this conversation. The road to education reform is long, but I know now that it is very much in our lifetimes.

Here's to the change that has already begun.

All my love,

Deborah Olatunji

APPENDIX

———

INTRODUCTION

National Center for Education Statistics. "Fast Facts: Back To School Statistics (372)." https://nces.ed.gov/fastfacts/display. asp?id=372 (accessed April 30, 2019.).

Robinson, Ken. "Do Schools Kill Creativity?" TED video, 19:22. Posted February 2006. https://www.ted.com/talks/sir_ken_robinson_do_schools_kill_creativity?language=en.

Workforce Career Readiness. "100 High Schoolers America Needs To Know About Class of 2019." https://www.workforcecareers.net/pages/about-us/100highschoolers2020 (accessed April 30, 2019.).

CHAPTER ONE

Andrews, Evan. "Reign Of Terror | History, Significance, & Facts." Encyclopædia Britannica. https://www.britannica.com/event/Reign-of-Terror. (accessed February 24, 2019.)

CHAPTER TWO

Dalile, Lily. "How Schools Are Killing Creativity." Huffpost. com. https://www.huffpost.com/entry/a-dictator-racing-to-nowh_b_1409138. (accessed March 13, 2019.)

Naiman, Linda. "What Is Creativity? (And Why Is It A Crucial Factor For Business Success?)" Creativity At Work. https://www.creativityatwork.com/2014/02/17/what-is-creativity/. (accessed March 13, 2019.)

Rein, Abi. "Cellular Respiration - Lessons." Tes Teach With Blendspace. https://www.tes.com/lessons/jdJhu2NGpiaoJQ/cellular-respiration. (accessed March 13, 2019.)

CHAPTER THREE

Horowitz, Juliana Menasce and Nikki Graf. "Most U.S. Teens See Anxiety, Depression As Major Problems." Pew Research Center's Social & Demographic Trends Project. https://www.pewsocialtrends.org/2019/02/20/most-u-s-teens-see-anxiety-and-depression-as-a-major-problem-among-their-peers/. (accessed March 13, 2019.)

Martin, Jamie. "Homeschooling 101: What Is Homeschooling?" *Parents*, 2012. https://www.parents.com/kids/education/home-schooling/homeschooling-101-what-is-homeschooling/. (accessed March 13, 2019.)

Poth, Rachelle D. "Personalized Learning Experiences: Why? And How?" Getting Smart. https://www.getting-smart.com/2018/03/personalized-learning-experiences-why-and-how/. (accessed March 13, 2019.)

Ray, Dr. Brian D. "Number Of Homeschoolers In U.S. 2017-2018 Home School Growing." National Home Education Research Institute. https://www.nheri.org/homeschool-population-size-growing/. (accessed March 13, 2019.)

Smith, Alex. "Minnesota Student Will Graduate With High School Diploma — And Nursing Degree." Star Tribune. http://www.startribune.com/minnesota-student-will-graduate-with-high-school-diploma-and-nursing-degree/510069072/?refresh=true. (accessed March 13, 2019.)

CHAPTER FOUR

Alexander, Michelle. "The New Jim Crow Context." Course Hero. https://www.coursehero.com/lit/The-New-Jim-Crow/context/. (accessed May 15, 2019.)

Broderick, James A. and Jill A. Broderick. "February 12, 1968: Black Sanitation Workers Strike In Memphis." Rhapsody In Books Weblog. https://rhapsodyinbooks.wordpress.com/2009/02/12/february-12-1968-black-sanitation-workers-strike-in-memphis/. (accessed December 12, 2019.)

Brown, DeNeen. "'I Am a Man': The ugly Memphis sanitation workers' strike that led to MLK's assassination." Washington Post. https://www.washingtonpost.com/news/retropolis/wp/2018/02/12/i-am-a-man-the-1968-memphis-sanitation-workers-strike-that-led-to-mlks-assassination/?noredirect=on. (accessed May 15, 2019.)

Estes, Steve. "'I am a Man!': Race, Masculinity, and the 1968 Memphis Sanitation Strike." *Labor History* 41, no. 2

(2000): 153-170. url: https://www.tandfonline.com/doi/
abs/10.1080/00236560050009914

Morland, Kenneth J. "Token Desegregation and Beyond." Crm-
vet.Org. https://www.crmvet.org/docs/63_src_school-de-
seg-r.pdf. (accessed May 15, 2019.)

Teaching Tolerance. "Introducing 'The New Jim Crow.'" https://
www.tolerance.org/classroom-resources/tolerance-lessons/
introducing-the-new-jim-crow. (accessed May 15, 2019.)

VisualImagesMedia. "I AM | Deborah Olatunji." YouTube, July
2, 2018. https://www.youtube.com/watch?v=0So4KHJXui4.

CHAPTER FIVE
Kagan, Julia. "Glass Ceiling." Investopedia. https://www.
investopedia.com/terms/g/glass-ceiling.asp. (accessed May
15, 2019.)

CHAPTER SIX
Cooper, Belle Beth. "The Science Of Failure: Why Highly Successful People Crave Mistakes." Resources. https://buffer.
com/resources/why-highly-successful-people-crave-failure-
and-mistakes. (accessed June 12, 2019.)

Mertz, Jon. "Activate Leadership – A Calling." Bing video,
02:22. Posted January 2015. https://www.bing.com/
videos/search?q=jon+mertz&&view=detail&mid=54E-
51937972A57475EC754E51937972A57475EC7&&FORM=VRD-
GAR.

Pontefract, Dan. "The Foolishness Of Fail Fast, Fail Often." *Forbes*, September 15, 2018. https://www.forbes.com/sites/danpontefract/2018/09/15/the-foolishness-of-fail-fast-fail-often/#6264239659d9. (accessed June 12, 2019.)

Singju, Pangambam. "Barbara Corcoran: Rethinking Failure At TedxBarnardCollege (Transcript)." The Singju Post. https://singjupost.com/barbara-corcoran-rethinking-failure-at-tedxbarnardcollege-transcript/. (accessed June 12, 2019.)

CHAPTER SEVEN

Bidwell, Allie. "Students Spend More Time on Homework but Teachers Say It's Worth It." *U.S. News and World Report*, February 27, 2014. https://www.usnews.com/news/articles/2014/02/27/students-spend-more-time-on-homework-but-teachers-say-its-worth-it. (accessed June 13, 2019.)

Gurumurthy, Rupa and Kendra Straley, et al. "Rote Memorization Vs. Critical Thinking: How Online Math Tutors Help." Thinkster Math. https://hellothinkster.com/blog/rote-learning-vs-critical-thinking-online-math-tutor-can-help/. (accessed June 13, 2019.)

Levy, Sandra and Dr. Karen Gill. "Is Too Much Homework Bad for Kids' Health?" Healthline. https://www.healthline.com/health-news/children-more-homework-means-more-stress-031114#1. (accessed June 13, 2019.)

Orlin, Ben. "When Memorization Gets In The Way Of Learning." *The Atlantic*, September 9, 2013. https://www.

theatlantic.com/education/archive/2013/09/when-memori-zation-gets-in-the-way-of-learning/279425/. (accessed June 13, 2019.)

Robinson, Ken. "Bring On The Learning Revolution!" TED video, 17:51. Posted February 2010. https://www.ted.com/talks/sir_ken_robinson_bring_on_the_learning_revolution/transcript.

Youthtruth. "Learning From Student Voice: Are Students Engaged?" https://youthtruthsurvey.org/student-engagement/#section1. (accessed June 13, 2019.)

CHAPTER EIGHT

Duke, Nell K. and Anne-Lise Halvorsen. "New Study Shows The Impact Of PBL On Student Achievement." Edutopia. https://www.edutopia.org/article/new-study-shows-impact-pbl-student-achievement-nell-duke-anne-lise-halvorsen. (accessed June 14, 2019.)

Jones, Abigail. "Murder Town USA (aka Wilmington, Delaware)." *Newsweek,* December 9, 2014. https://www.newsweek.com/2014/12/19/wilmington-delaware-murder-crime-290232.html. (accessed June 14, 2019.)

Milatz, Anne, Marko Lüftenegger, and Barbara Schober. "Teachers' Relationship Closeness With Students As A Resource For Teacher Wellbeing: A Response Surface Analytical Approach." *Frontiers In Psychology* 6(2015): 1949. url: doi:10.3389/fpsyg.2015.01949.

Teach & Kids Learn (TKL). "Does Project-Based Learning Increase Student Learning? What Does Research Say?" https://www.teachnkidslearn.com/does-pbl-increase-student-learning/. (accessed June 14, 2019.)

The Educator's Room. "How Students Lose When Teachers Become The Enemy." https://theeducatorsroom.com/how-students-lose-when-teachers-become-the-enemy/. (accessed June 14, 2019.)

CHAPTER NINE

Clayton, Sarah. "These Are The Subjects That Should ACTU-ALLY Be Taught In Secondary Schools." Lovin.ie. https://lovin.ie/opinion/these-are-the-subjects-that-should-actually-be-taught-in-secondary-schools. (accessed June 23, 2019.)

Do Something. "11 Facts About High School Dropout Rates." https://www.dosomething.org/us/facts/11-facts-about-high-school-dropout-rates#fn1. (accessed June 23, 2019.)

Juliani, A.J. "The 20% Project (Like Google) In My Class." http://ajjuliani.com/the-20-project-like-google-in-my-class/. (accessed June 23, 2019.)

Stopera, Dave. "Less Than 35% Of Americans Can Name Every State In 4 Minutes, Can You?" Buzzfeed, February 27, 2019. https://www.buzzfeed.com/daves4/state-timed-quiz-minutes. (accessed June 23, 2019.)

CHAPTER TEN

Capaldi, Edward. "What is Moonshot Thinking." YouTube, September 13, 2017. https://www.youtube.com/watch?v=pEr-4j8kgwOk.

Grant, Adam (@AdamMGrant). "Don't ask kids what." Twitter, April 3, 2019. https://twitter.com/AdamMGrant/status/1113410148180078592.

Grissom, Jason A., Luis A. Rodriguez, and Emily C. Kern. "Teacher And Principal Diversity And The Representation Of Students Of Color In Gifted Programs: Evidence From National Data." *The Elementary School Journal* 117, no. 3 (2017): 396-422. url: https://www.journals.uchicago.edu/doi/abs/10.1086/690274.

Haskell, Kristie. "Preparing Students For Life?" National Association of Independent Schools. https://www.nais.org/magazine/independent-school/spring-2014/preparing-students-for-life/. (accessed June 25, 2019.)

Kinseth, Amanda. "Digital Future: The Youtuber Age - What Kids Want To Be When They Grow Up." WPDE. https://wpde.com/news/local/digital-future-the-youtuber-age-what-kids-want-to-be-when-they-grow-up. (accessed June 25, 2019.)

Lawson, Kimberly. "Why Seeing Yourself Represented On Screen Is So Important." *VICE,* February 20, 2018. https://www.vice.com/en_us/article/zmwq3x/why-diversity-on-screen-is-important-black-panther. (accessed June 25, 2019.)

Lindsay, Constance A. and Cassandra M. D. Hart. "Exposure To Same-Race Teachers And Student Disciplinary Outcomes For Black Students In North Carolina." *SAGE Journals* 39, no. 3 (2017): 485-510. url: https://journals.sagepub.com/doi/abs/10.3102/0162373717693109.

Olatunji, Miracle. *Purpose: How To Live and Lead With Impact.* New Degree Press, 2019.

National Association of Colleges and Employers. "Career Readiness Defined." https://www.naceweb.org/career-readiness/competencies/career-readiness-defined/. (accessed June 25, 2019.)

Usability.Gov. "Prototyping." https://www.usability.gov/how-to-and-tools/methods/prototyping.html. (accessed June 25, 2019.)

CHAPTER ELEVEN

Micheletti, Gabrielle. "Re-Envisioning Paulo Freire's 'Banking Concept Of Education.'" *Inquiries Journal* 2, no. 2 (2010): 1. url: http://www.inquiriesjournal.com/articles/171/re-envisioning-paulo-freires-banking-concept-of-education.

Tomaka, Lauren. "States In Region Investing More In Apprenticeship Programs." The Council of State Governments. https://www.csgmidwest.org/policyresearch/0114apprenticeship.aspx. (accessed June 27, 2019.)

CHAPTER TWELVE

Collins Dictionary. "Character Definition And Meaning." https://www.collinsdictionary.com/dictionary/english/character. (accessed June 28, 2019.)

Duckworth, Angela. "Grit: The power of passion and perseverance." TED video, 6:07. Posted April 2013. https://www.ted.com/talks/angela_lee_duckworth_grit_the_power_of_passion_and_perseverance?language=en.

CHAPTER THIRTEEN

Bacon, Jono. "The Art Of Community, Second Edition." O'Reilly | Safari Books Online.

https://www.oreilly.com/library/view/the-art-of/9781449337506/ch01.html. (accessed June 29, 2019.)

Dastagir, Alia E. "Microaggressions don't just 'hurt your feelings.'" USA Today, February 28, 2018. https://www.usatoday.com/story/news/2018/02/28/what-microaggressions-small-slights-serious-consequences/362754002/. (accessed June 29, 2019).

Daum, Kevin. "7 Things You Have To Do To Build A Powerful Community." Inc., February 17, 2017. https://www.inc.com/kevin-daum/7-things-you-have-to-do-to-build-a-powerful-community.html. (accessed June 29, 2019.)

OECD Insights: Human Capital. "What is social capital?" Organisation for Economic Co-operation and Development.

https://www.oecd.org/insights/37966934.pdf. (accessed June 29, 2019.)

Onnit. "400 Trillion To One | Gary Vaynerchuk." YouTube, May 30, 2017. https://www.youtube.com/watch?v=JCvqyFd6ux-k&feature=emb_title.

Schaps, Eric. "Creating A School Community." *Educational Leadership* 60, no. 6 (2003): 31-33. url: http://www.ascd.org/publications/educational-leadership/mar03/vol60/num06/Creating-a-School-Community.aspx.

CHAPTER FOURTEEN

Liu, Antonia. *Hack College Like An Entrepreneur: 40 Surprising Insights from the World's Top Founders.* New Degree Press, 2017.

Ramos, Yuritzy. "College Students Tend To Change Majors When They Find The One They Really Love." *Borderzine*, March 15, 2013. https://borderzine.com/2013/03/college-students-tend-to-change-majors-when-they-find-the-one-they-really-love/. (accessed June 30, 2019.)

CHAPTER FIFTEEN

DECA Inc. "About Page." https://www.deca.org/about/. (accessed September 3, 2019.)

First-Arai, Leanna. "This 16-Year-Old Is Taking The School Climate Strike To The U.S. Capitol." *YES! Magazine*, May 24, 2019. https://www.yesmagazine.org/planet/cli-

mate-strike-american-capitol-student-20190524. (accessed
September 3, 2019.)

Hill, Rebecca. "The Rise Of Science Fairs (And Why They
Matter)." Parentmap. https://www.parentmap.com/article/
stream-stem-science-fair-prizes. (accessed September 3,
2019.)

Mackie, Mubeen. "Why Is Growth Hacking Important For
A Startup?" Thiken. https://medium.com/thiken/why-is-
growth-hacking-important-for-a-startup-9f2abeffof73.
(accessed September 3, 2019.)

The DICE Initiative. "Our Beliefs." https://www.dicei.org/.
(accessed September 3, 2019.)

Volcano Discovery. "Latest Earthquakes In Oklahoma, USA /
List And Interactive Map: Past 7 Days." https://www.volca-
nodiscovery.com/earthquakes/oklahoma.html. (accessed
September 3, 2019.)

CHAPTER SIXTEEN

Almendrala, Anna. "5 Signs You Were Raised By Helicopter Parents." Huffpost. https://www.huffpost.com/
entry/5-ways-to-tell-you-were-raised-by-helicopter-par-
ents_n_5609de6ee4b0dd850308e260. (accessed November 7,
2019.)

ClassTag Team. "How To Reach Parents Who Don't Seem To
Care About Education." Classtag. https://blog.classtag.com/

reach-parents-who-dont-care-about-education/. (accessed November 7, 2019.)

Dinan, Stephen. "English isn't main language at home for 21 percent in America." *The Washington Times,* October 6, 2015. https://www.washingtontimes.com/news/2015/oct/6/english-isnt-main-language-at-home-for-21-in-ameri/. (accessed November 7, 2019.)

University of Delaware Cooperative Extension. "How Parents Can Help Their Kids Be Successful In School." University of Delaware. https://www.udel.edu/canr/cooperative-extension/fact-sheets/parents-help-children-school-success/. (accessed November 7, 2019.)

Waterford. "How Parent Involvement Leads To Student Success." https://www.waterford.org/education/how-parent-involvment-leads-to-student-success/. (accessed November 7, 2019.)

CHAPTER SEVENTEEN

American Red Cross. "First Aid Steps | Perform First Aid." Red Cross. https://www.redcross.org/take-a-class/first-aid/performing-first-aid/first-aid-steps. (accessed November 14, 2019.)

Amstrong, Brian. "8 Essential Skills They Didn't Teach You In School." Lifehack. https://www.lifehack.org/articles/lifestyle/8-essential-skills-they-didnt-teach-you-in-school.html. (accessed November 14, 2019.)

Babauta, Leo. "9 Eternally Vital Life Skills (That They Don't Teach In School)." Highexistence. https://highexistence. com/9-eternally-vital-life-skills-that-they-dont-teach-you-in-school/. (accessed November 14, 2019.)

Bariso, Justin. "Bill Gates Follows These 4 Rules To Get The Most From His Reading." *Inc.*, November 21, 2017. https:// www.inc.com/justin-bariso/bill-gates-follows-4-rules-to-get-most-from-reading-books.html. (accessed November 14, 2019.)

Breslin, Susannah. "How To Sell Yourself." *Forbes,* June 8, 2012. https://www.forbes.com/sites/susannahbreslin/2012/06/08/how-to-sell-yourself/#62524d316843. (accessed November 14, 2019.)

Bruce, Kalen. "47 Things You Weren't Taught In School (That Our Kids Need To Know)." Freedom Sprout. https://freedomsprout.com/things-schools-dont-teach/. (accessed November 14, 2019.)

Bruce, Kalen. "15 Finance Terms Children Need To Understand." Freedom Sprout. https://freedomsprout.com/finance-terms-for-children/. (accessed November 14, 2019.)

Bruce, Kalen. "The Need For Children's Financial Education." Freedom Sprout. https://freedomsprout.com/childrens-financial-education/. (accessed November 14, 2019.)

Mahan, Lori. "Banzai." *Saratoga Today,* October 12, 2017. https:// www.saratogatodaynewspaper.com/today-in-saratoga/education/item/7377-banzai. (accessed November 14, 2019.)

Marr, Bernard. "5 Vital Skills Schools Are Failing To Teach Well Enough." *Forbes,* October 4, 2016. https://www.forbes.com/sites/bernardmarr/2016/10/04/5-vital-skills-schools-are-failing-to-teach-well-enough/#69a17a3e106a. (accessed November 14, 2019.)

Narcan. "What Is NARCAN® (Naloxone) Nasal Spray." ADAPT Pharma, Inc. https://www.narcan.com/. (accessed November 14, 2019.)

Shaw, Gina and Dr. Brunilda Nazario. "Water And Stress Reduction: Sipping Stress Away." WebMD. https://www.webmd.com/diet/features/water-stress-reduction#1. (accessed November 14, 2019.)

Sicinski, Adam. "Six Ideas For How To Build A Loving Relationship." IQ Doodle. https://iqdoodle.com/loving-relationship/. (accessed November 14, 2019.)

Smith, Jacquelyn. "5 Ways To Sell Yourself In A Job Interview." *Business Insider,* May 11, 2015. https://www.businessinsider.com/how-to-sell-yourself-in-an-interview-2015-5. (accessed November 14, 2019.)

Thorn, Beverly, et.al. "Healthy Ways To Handle Life's Stressors." American Psychological Association. https://www.apa.org/topics/stress-tips. (accessed November 14, 2019.)

Zhu, Jessie. 2017. "What Is Self-Awareness And Why Is It Important? [+5 Ways To Increase It]." Positive Psychology. https://positivepsychology.com/self-awareness-matters-how-you-can-be-more-self-aware/. (accessed November 14, 2019.)

CHAPTER EIGHTEEN

First Round. "We Studied 100 Mentor-Mentee Matches — Here's What Makes Mentorship Work." https://firstround.com/review/we-studied-100-mentor-mentee-matches-heres-what-makes-mentorship-work/. (accessed November 15, 2019.)

Kaiser Family Foundation. "Population Distribution By Age." https://www.kff.org/other/state-indicator/distribution-by-age/?dataView=1&currentTimeframe=0&selectedDistributions=children-0-18&sortModel=%7B%22colId%22:%22Location%22,%22sort%22:%22asc%22%7D. (accessed November 15, 2019.)

Mueller, Sarah. "State Lawmakers Plan To Require Schools To Provide Students Free Sanitary Products." *Delaware Public Media*, October 18, 2019. https://www.delawarepublic.org/post/state-lawmakers-plan-require-schools-provide-students-free-sanitary-products. (accessed November 15, 2019.)

Olatunji, Dorcas. "A Teen's Tribute To The Delaware Orgs Guiding Her Along The Startup Path." *Technical.ly Delaware*, August 29, 2019. https://technical.ly/delaware/2019/08/29/dorcas-olatunji-teens-tribute-to-delaware-youth-programs-entrepreneurship-startup-journey/. (accessed November 15, 2019.)

Sasson, Remez. "How Many Thoughts Does Your Mind Think In One Hour?" Success Consciousness. https://www.successconsciousness.com/blog/inner-peace/how-many-thoughts-does-your-mind-think-in-one-hour/. (accessed November 15, 2019.)

TEDx Talks. "Defaulting to Yes | Catherine Lindroth | TEDxYouth@IndependenceSchool." YouTube, April 14, 2017. https://www.youtube.com/watch?v=RHJI6b1JgZM.

Tjan, Anthony. "What The Best Mentors Do." 2017. *Harvard Business Review,* February 27, 2017. https://hbr.org/2017/02/what-the-best-mentors-do. (accessed November 15, 2019.)

Wright, Michelle. "The Three C's Of Mentorship." Ye!. https://yecommunity.com/ar/blog/how-mentors-bring-advice-to-mentorship. (accessed November 15, 2019.)

Made in the USA
Columbia, SC
27 February 2020